Dressage Principles Illuminated
Expanded Edition

by Charles de Kunffy

XENOPHON PRESS

Dressage Principles Illuminated, Expanded Softcover Edition 2024
Charles de Kunffy

First published in 2002 as *Dressage Principles Illuminated* by Trafalgar Square Publishing

North Pomfret, Vermont 05053

Copyright © 2002 Charles de Kunffy

All rights reserved. No part of this book may be reproduced, by any means, without written permission of the publisher, except by a reviewer quoting brief excerpts for a review in a magazine, newspaper, or web site.

Any use of this publication to train generative artificial intelligence ("AI") technologies is expressly prohibited. The author and publisher reserve all rights to license uses of this work for generative AI training and development of machine learning language models.

The author has made every effort to obtain releases from all persons appearing in the photographs used in this book and all photographers. In some cases, however, the person's and photographer's identities and whereabouts were unknown. Should any names become available, they will be credited in future editions, assuming permission is granted.

Disclaimer:
The author and publisher shall have neither liability nor responsibility to any person or entity with respect to any loss or damage caused or alleged to be caused directly or indirectly by the information contained in this book. While the book is as accurate as the author can make it, there may be errors, omissions, and inaccuracies.

Library of Congress Cataloging-in-Publication Data De Kunffy, Charles
Dressage Principles Illuminated / Charles de Kunffy.
ISBN 1570762333 (first edition hardcover)
1. Dressage. I. Title.
SF309.5 .D442 2002 798.2'3—dc21
2002007551

Dressage Principles Illuminated Expanded Edition

Xenophon Press Softcover Edition ISBN: 978-1948717588 Copyright 2024
Xenophon Press eBook Edition ISBN: 978-1948717595 Copyright 2024
Xenophon Press Collector's Edition ISBN: 978-1948717250 Copyright 2021

Franktown, Virginia USA
XenophonPress@gmail.com
www.XenophonPress.com

Dressage Principles Illuminated
Expanded Edition

by Charles de Kunffy

Media by Charles de Kunffy:
A Rider's Survival from Tyranny
Creative Horsemanship
Dressage Principles Illuminated Expanded Edition
Dressage Questions Answered
The Art of Traditional Dressage DVD
The Athletic Development of the Dressage Horse
The Ethics and Passions of Dressage Expanded Edition

Contents

List of Illustrations . . . ix
Dedication . . . xiii
Acknowledgments. . . xv
Preface. . . xvii

Part 1: Introduction . . . 1
Chapter 1 The Horse and Rider Partnership . . . 3
Chapter 2 The Classical Tradition . . . 15
Chapter 3 Classical versus Competitive Riding . . . 22

Part 2: Training the horse . . . 31
Chapter 4 The Nature of the Horse . . . 33
Chapter 5 Training Principles . . . 39
Chapter 6 Rehabilitative Work . . . 47
Chapter 7 Therapeutic Work . . . 62
Chapter 8 Athletic Development . . . 69

Part 3: Training the rider . . . 77
Chapter 9 What It Means to Be an Equestrian . . . 79
Chapter 10 The Role of Teachers . . . 83
Chapter 11 The Rider's Position and Aids . . . 90
Chapter 12 Schooling Ideologies . . . 107

Recommended Reading . . . 115

Xenophon Press Library . . . 117

List of Illustrations and Credits

1.1, Hero's Monument – The author . . . 3
1.2, Piaffe – Richard Malmgren . . . 7
1.3, Half-pass left – Richard Malmgren . . . 9
1.4, Palais Belvedere – The author . . . 13
2.1 & 2.2, Geza Hazslinszky-Krull – Courtesy Carolyn von Schaik . . . 16
2.3, Colonel Josipovich – Unknown . . . 19
3.0, Correct posture in competition Richard Malmgren . . . 23
3.1, Transition from Collected to Medium Canter – Richard Malmgren . . . 25
3.2, Correctly Stretched Horse – The author & Beth Preston . . . 27
3.3, Roll Kur – The author and Beth Preston . . . 27
3.4 a & b, Gyula Dallos and Aktion – Unknown . . . 29
4.0, The Carriage of the Horse's Neck – Richard Malmgren . . . 35
5.0 a & b, Piaffe – Richard Malmgren . . . 39
5.0 c, Medium Trot - Richard Malmgren . . . 40
5.1 a–f, The Range of Trot Possibilities – Martha Cardon Irmer . . . 43-44
5.2, Escape Mechanisms and Remedies – Chart by the author . . . 46
6.0, Canter "Strike Off" – Richard Malmgren . . . 48
6.1 a & b, Extended Trot – Courtesy Arthur Kottas-Heldenberg . . . 50
6.2, Yielding the Rein – Virginia Elder . . . 52
6.3 a, Full Yield in the Medium Trot – Walter Roll . . . 53
6.3 b, Stretching the Horse "long and low" – Kevin Berne . . . 53
6.4 a & b, Raising the Horse's Back – Susan Wingate . . . 58

6.5 a & b, Uphill Balance – Sheri Scott . . . 59

7.1 a & b, The Authority of the Seat in Trot – Courtesy Arthur Kottas-Heldenberg . . . 63

7.2 a & b, Effectiveness and Symmetry of the Seat – Susan Wingate . . . 65

7.3 a & b, Riding with Positioning – Courtesy Arthur Kottas-Heldenberg . . . 67

7.4 a & b, Riding in "Functional Straightness" – Kevin Berne . . . 68

8.1, Vocabulary of Daily Work – The author . . . 70

8.2 a & b, Bending as an Act of "Straightening" – Martha Cardon Irmer . . . 71

8.3 a & b, "Bursts" into Medium Trot – Richard Malmgren . . . 72

10.1 a, Common Problems of the Seat – The author and Beth Preston . . . 84

10.1 b, A Remedy for the Seat – The author and Beth Preston . . . 85

10.2, "Sculpting" the Rider – Kevin Berne . . . 87

10.3 a, Longeing in Groups – Kevin Berne . . . 89

10.3 b, Combining Longeing Exercises – Kevin Berne . . . 89

11.1, Chair Exercises for Developing a Seat – Drawing by Sandy Rabinowitz . . . 92

11.2 a–h, Leg Position – Richard F. Williams . . . 93-95

11.3 a, Full Yield on the Inside Rein – Kevin Berne . . . 98

11.3 b, Functionally Straight on the Diagonal – Kevin Berne . . . 98

11.4, Medium Trot on the Circle – Susan Wingate . . . 99

11.5 a, The Halt – Janet Newis . . . 100

11.5 b, The Halt – Kevin Berne . . . 100

11.6 a & b, Haunches-In – Courtesy Arthur-Kottas Heldenberg . . . 103

11.7 a–c, Shoulder-In, Positioning, and Bending – Janet Newis . . . 104-105

12.1. Role of the Rider's Legs – Chart by the author . . . 107

12.2, Collected Canter – Janet Newis . . . 108

Publisher's Introduction

Xenophon Press is pleased to present this softcover edition of what many followers of Charles de Kunffy consider to be their "bible." Since our publication of the collector's edition in 2021, riders and trainers alike have asked for a more portable version. This text is a favorite of riders and trainers alike and stands as a cornerstone of Charles' writings: *to treat our horses with dignity, respect and kindness*. This edition will be treasured and referred to often. The chapters are succinct, and cover essential topics that need to be embedded in the minds of riders and trainers.

We encourage you to read, and re-read the material, study the diagrams, photos, and method. I would like to thank Mary Fleishman sincerely for her valuable copy editing suggestions. For those of us fortunate enough to have studied and taught with Charles, this volume serves as a valuable reminder of his decades of dedicated pedagogy.

We hope you will enjoy this book and, just as importantly, share or gift it to other riders that you care about.

Here's to fostering mindful, classical riding,

Richard F. Williams
Editor-in-Chief
Publisher
Xenophon Press

Dedication

This book is a thank you to all of the fabulous riding instructors who taught me, and to all of my students who continue to inspire me.

Acknowledgments

I am indebted to too many horsemen and women to name them all here. However, in this book, I refer to some of my wonderful teachers. I was awestruck in their presence. You will also see pictures of admired colleagues, students, and riders. In addition, many great riders and authors have tutored my mind, and inspired my spirit. This book is written with gratitude to them all.

Those riders who contributed their beautiful pictures are named in the captions, and those who patiently and expertly photographed them are listed in the Table of Illustrations. I am grateful to all of you. This edition of my book is expanded, edited and redesigned by Xenophon Press. I wish to thank my publisher, Richard F. Williams for editing this new expanded edition including the entire text, new captions and images. With his encouragement, we expanded on the original topics and added sections and new images and a contemporary design.

Charles de Kunffy
Palm Springs
June 2021

Preface

This book is dedicated to the advocacy of the classical equestrian tradition.

This tradition is based on time-honored riding and training principles, all of which can be studied and understood. Equitation is labeled "classical" when it embodies the principles that have been tested and their results verified through the centuries.

Educated riders retained only those principles that worked with most horses for most riders, most effectively, most of the time. The classical principles of horsemanship are pragmatic and retain only the best of knowledge, leaving us the task to learn them. Toying with "new" or "innovative" riding methods and "techniques" amounts to wasteful diversion because it is experimentation with the discarded trials of thousands of riders who explored the same concepts centuries ago, long before we were born.

Although riders are eager to learn correct riding and training principles, they often fail to find good sources for acquiring them. With few exceptions, the traditional—often military—riding academies have ceased to exist and with their demise came the attrition of expertise held by the graduates of these once-great institutions. Yet, there continues to be a yearning for the learning of the principles that honor the horse and elevate his rider's character.

If equestrian experts become a minority among riders, and their number continues to diminish without arrangements for educating a new generation of experts, then the art, science, and scholarship of horsemanship will be threatened with irreparable loss.

Nothing is as liberating as knowledge. Expertise in a subject enables us to explain what we know with ease. For what we know, we can teach. That is how cultural development has always been possible. Once we learn the principles of an art or science and practice them in an honorable way, our expertise becomes recognized by other experts in the same field.

At the same time, there exists a perception of vagueness about the equestrian arts and that contributes to the dangerous opinion that expertise can be measured by different yardsticks, the most commonly accepted, of which might well be based on success in competition. Such success is worthy of admiration, but it cannot be accepted as evidence of equestrian expertise. Undeniably, riders may succeed in competition—a highly specialized activity—without necessarily being part of the traditional equestrian culture or possessing substantial knowledge.

The problem of understanding this is increased by false analogies drawn between horsemanship and other sports in which competitive success is, and should be the only measurement of prestige and standing. Those who understand the history of the equestrian tradition will realize that competition became part of it only in its very recent history—about a hundred years ago. Ever since its appearance as a great motivating force for the growth of the riding sport, competition never proved to have any merit in ranking true equestrian knowledge. Some of the greatest riders in the world do not compete. Some of the finest riders may be under-horsed and do not succeed in competitions although they ride well in them. I know that many excellent riders I either taught or judged in competition did not ride great horses and therefore could not out score lesser riders on better horses in contests. Ultimately, riding skills, scholarship and personal attributes, not competition scores, should matter in ranking riders.

Students of riding who understand riding theory will always excel at its practice. Instructors and judges can quickly discern and identify those who have studied and understood equestrian theory. In fact, riders without theoretical knowledge cannot even be instructed successfully.

Those who understand the equestrian culture, with its age-old principles of good equitation and admirable schooling of horses, can contribute to its continued health. Only riders who understand the systematic, gradual development of riding skills can practice and teach them. Equally important, the gymnastic development of the horse will successfully result in a supple and collected horse only as a byproduct of the rider's academic understanding. Only those riders who understand the definition of each concept involved in equestrian life can communicate with one another about it meaningfully.

With this book, I hope to contribute to the understanding of good horsemanship.

Part 1:
Introduction

Chapter 1
The Horse and Rider Partnership

Thousands of years ago, man tamed the horse, and as a result, we experience thrills and pleasures that few advances in technology have been able to duplicate. Indeed, it was man's craving for more strength and speed than evolution had allotted him that motivated his desire to tame horses. Indeed, it was man's self-centeredness and vanity that inspired the patronage and sponsorship that, in turn, enabled the creation of so much beauty in the world.

With horses, where random nature was found, man recognized it as raw material that could be useful, if properly altered, to suit human aesthetic needs. The result was the birth of art.

However, and perhaps unexpectedly, the horse repaid man's efforts to tame and teach him by both elevating the character, and strengthening the virtue of the people who came into contact with him. The tamer of the horse became his pupil. His rider, elevated well above ground by him, was raised in spirit and also in character. This is evidenced in countless equestrian monuments. A ruler, a conqueror, adventurer, a leader of pedestrian people, all are portrayed enthroned on horseback. Out of respect for the horse's ability to elevate the virtuous above the common people, we must always remain humbled by our privileged position as riders (fig. 1.1).

FIGURE 1.1 *The statues of the Seven chieftains of the Magyars on Heroes' Square, in Budapest, was begun for the millennial celebration of Hungarian nationhood, in 1896 and mostly complete by 1900. These men on horseback are some of the seven tribal chiefs that led their tribes into the Carpathian Basin. They are grouped behind their leader, Arpad [at left], who founded the first Hungarian Royal House. This monument presents a wonderful herd of horses on whose backs these powerful conquerors were enthroned.*

People who are taught by other people can simply pick and choose what is delectable to their tastes. When receiving an education from a horse, this is not possible. Horses teach their lessons by subjecting their riders to firsthand experiences that cannot be selectively denied. *Horses form their riders from within and foster the development of courage, humility, quickness of judgment, self-discipline, self-control, and focus. They encourage the wondrous attitude of empathy*, so at odds with the selfishness in mankind.

Learning from horses is compulsory for riders, and those who resist it will suffer the consequences of ignorance through pain and damage.

And so it came to pass that after man tamed the horse, he came to desire to change his character, looks, and abilities by selective breeding. Man succeeded in diversifying the horse to suit his various needs and created many different beautiful breeds within the species. This effort brought wealth through diversity and opportunity through variety. Riders have the opportunity to gain wisdom by learning skills necessary to ride any horse. Those who can control only a few horses, or only a small subset of horses, and with those, only to a limited extent, are not yet fully developed equestrians.

Monotony goes against human impulses, and in that, we find the heart of equestrian pleasures. No two moments on the back of a horse are identical. Every horse in every minute offers us a gift as novel and unexpected as any we have ever seen. When riding, the thrill is in the novelty, the adventure, the discovery of the inimitable.

A grazing animal with a deceptive appearance of docility, the horse can flare into flames of fire when alerted by flights of fancy that will test his proven powers to gain ground swiftly. Just as he outran his enemies, he galloped into human hearts, taking away the breath of men who, in ancient times, were themselves already dreaming of flight. And so it was, and so will it remain that everything about the horse has a seeming duality. Within seconds, the gentle companion can suddenly turn dangerous, his heavy weight becoming devastatingly destructive as he is prompted to flight by his instinct to survive.

It took thousands of years to craft the vocabulary with which we could convey our wishes to the horse, and it took equally long to listen to his messages in silent meditation.

Riders have the duty and an obligation to their equine teachers to make sure that these seamless, secret languages— that allow the flow of thought from man to horse and the flow of energy from horse to man—will continue to be passed on to others. The rider must bear witness that horse and rider remain in conversation, exchanging human thoughts for equine energy which, when altered by the rider, will appear as new wellsprings of the mutual joy of both horse and rider. Horse and rider take flight together, the intelligent partner in control and the strong one the supplier of his wondrous power and energy.

Few undertakings by man have been more artful than the taming and riding of the horse. Man can take random nature and transform it into art, but only a horseman can add the aspect of lending himself to participation in creating art by communion, becoming, incidentally, the creator of art in which he is both object and subject of self-made beauty. Horse and rider, united by purpose and harmonious in motion, together create art that is far more inspired and beautiful than either could achieve without the other.

Michelangelo's masterpiece, the Sistine Chapel, appears to have been effortless, provided it is seen as a mere mixing of colors and the painting of a decorative ceiling and walls. Yet, it is one of the great wonders of the world. Michelangelo's genius had to control inanimate and innate materials to achieve his art. The rider must control artistic materials that are willful and living: the temper of the rider and the extravagant energy of his horse. The rider's art has dimensions that those in the fine arts do not have to struggle with. The willful horse must be transformed into a willing, living object of art, and must be so perceived while in great animation and at the disposal of his rider. The riding art will not be complete as a painting is at the moment when the painter "puts down his brush," but rather continues dynamically both in spirit and body until the rider wills it to rest. The art of riding is never complete, it merely pauses. A respite for another day, another hour, another minute brings forth all that amounts to different, fresh, and new art.

Riding as a Quest

Riding is a quest, not a conquest. It is a quest for perfection, which if it is properly defined in the rider's mind, cannot be achieved. The rider rests with that thought, knowing that the quest for perfection brings its own glories. Those who are pursuing the conquest of the horse will fail in their art, for the horse will either rightfully revolt or submit with docility to despicable slavery, which instantly renders him eminently unattractive. Those who ride for conquest over horses seek self-glorification and fame—the small currency of childish people.

The German poet, Novalis, said, "Every disease is a musical disorder. Every cure is a musical solution." I find that riding, which depends so much on precision of rhythm, seamless flow of motion and interaction based on emotional awareness, is a musical activity in many ways. While music may well be the most unnecessary necessity of life, it is a great source of pleasure and and inspiration to all of us. Particularly from a rider's point of view, we ought to understand that in music the silence is as important as the notes. So it is in riding that the times of introspective passivity in harmony with the horse's action are as important as the times giving the aids. The periods of musical silence are analogous to the rider's promotion of the status quo and the sounds are analogous to aiding influences for change. In the art of riding, as in music, there are periods of omission (silence) alternating with periods of commission (sounds). Riders who understand this can sensitize their horses to appear as if they read their rider's mind and hasten their eager compliance with their rider's wishes. Riders out of tune with their horses remain out of tune with many other things in life because the "musical dimension" of riding penetrates the very center of our character.

The wonders of riding are many, but perhaps the most important is an awareness of never-ending discovery. From moment to moment, riders experience various sensory perceptions, which when understood, analyzed and synthesized, help them discover more about their horse, the partner. Mindful of the horse's monitoring his rider in return, we must know that while the horse perceives no profound insights, he does, however, come to definitive conclusions about his rider, primarily by understanding the differences between pleasure and pain. As nature would have it, he revolts against pain and discomfort while gladly succumbing to pleasure.

Wise riders understand the value of focusing on another living creature. While in a state of anticipation, the rider can internalize discoveries about his horse's nature, behavior, character, and responses. The curious byproduct of the process of discovery and awareness of other living beings is that we react to them according to our own self-perceptions. Therefore, our responses highlight our own nature to ourselves. The pleasure in the art of riding comes with the thrill of self-discovery and insight. And so, it transpires that the rider receives, as one of his horse's many gifts, privileged access to information about himself without wallowing in harmfully self-indulgent self-analysis. Riders who focus on the well-being of their horse, rather than on childish self-indulgences, will grow significantly to a mature person, with an admirable character visible in a mirror held for him by his horse.

Man matures by outward orientation, not by inward focus and self-indulgence. It is through participating in relationships with others that our self emerges, becomes aware of its resources and powers, and roars to fulfillment. Loneliness is an ill adviser. By building a relationship with a horse, which by definition must be reciprocal, one fulfills the requirements for companionship. His spirit soaring, his intellect challenged, his communications confirmed and reflected by his horse, man stands in a relationship that cannot be duplicated by other humans. With the horse there is no deception, no contrivance, no double-crossing. Horses are never traitors and they lack the capacity to intellectualize in order to justify deplorable behavior. They represent admirable ethics without, of course, being aware of it. Horses have no designs on humans and are not predatory when recognizing the virtue in the rider's character. They take no unjust advantage.

As much as humans are trained to hide their emotions, horses will physically manifest them, instantaneously. When a horse is frightened, apprehensive, intimidated, shy, brave, heady, vivacious, or otherwise, these emotions instantly surface in physical display. Horses' emotions are "worn on their skin" by displaying physiological changes and different postures, and by instinctively prompted movements. We must maintain our ability to reprimand a horse with a smile or lavish rewards on him with a frown, while he's allowed to overwhelm our intellect and emotions with his physical spontaneity. These are some of the secrets behind our love of the thrills, which only horses can give us.

The rider is participating in creation, blending the complex ingredients of horse and rider, unlikely creatures for a harmonious partnership. Mixing the palette

FIGURE 1.2 *An attentive and relaxed horse in Piaffe. Haunches sinking forehand rising, posture generous and correct. Obvious display of the poll being the highest point with nose ahead of the eyes. Great confidence and energy. Jessica Jo Tate riding.*

constantly to adjust the elements of his art, the rider colors, shades, and shapes each moment with his horse. The rider is the maker of the beauty to be born of harmony, and he is part of the beautiful object that is to result from it. An unparalleled experience, comparable only to life itself, is the magic of perpetually giving birth to something new, something better, something more beautiful.

Riding as Discovery

In my life, riding has remained a guiding principle because of its constant analogy to life. Horses have taught me wonderful lessons, the most fundamental of which is that life is a perpetual discovery. The only constant in life is change. Life is ever changing, therefore inexorably dynamic. Events are lived the way we interpret them. Life, essentially, is lived in our minds. These observations about life are equally applicable to horsemanship, that is, the knowledge of horses and our interaction with them.

From time immemorial, man has worried about the meaning of life and has questioned why we are here and where we are going. Uncertainty sets in as a consequence of having no categorical answers.

If life is meant to be a journey of discovery, then riding is a metaphor for life. The motivating force that gives strength and stamina for the effort life demands is love. The more passionate it is, the more satisfaction it delivers. So, it is the love of horses and the passion for training them, which motivates good riders.

The rewards of riding include knowledge of particulars and wisdom derived from them. For truth is greater than the sum-total of particulars. And while truth is greater than facts, it cannot be discerned without analyzing facts. So it is with horses, horsemanship, and the art of riding.

Life becomes a torment if we think about it in terms of absolutes and finalities, rather than as a negotiable experience. The truth is that only ideals are absolute, and you should not feel pressured into having to achieve them. A life spent believing that one can turn ideals into reality can become a life spent in disappointment, or a life perceived as one of underachievement. Ideals must be known and studied; they ought to be guiding our aspirations but we must understand that we will never achieve them. These are also the lessons horsemanship teaches us. Life, much like riding, is always unfinished business. The process of discovering it should be the source of pleasure.

The beauty of life is in its mystery. If life were predictable, it would not be worth living. The mystery of life makes it worth living. The experience of riding is similar. It is based on the knowledge that the end is unpredictable, and the journey to it full of hazards. While riding, attention is focused on the ideals sought. Yet, as reality presents itself, the course to seeking them is re-charted. Good riders know that every moment contains an insight that concerns an ideal that will never be attained, but serves as the guiding light for the right effort.

Life, like riding, consists of interpreting its unavoidable events. The art of living depends on the interpretation of the inevitable and the attitudes that follow from gleaning insights from them. We should work with a horse, as we should conduct our life. First, perceive that is actually happening, then choose an appropriate response to it. "Appropriate" is a response motivated by love and resulting in knowledge. We must not think of riding as teaching horses a lesson. Rather, we should accept the notion that the horse teaches us lessons. We are simply allowed to love him, administer to his needs, and tutor him to unfold his many talents.

Good riding, like a life well lived, is grounded in self-discipline. A disciplined person has focus, concentration, and is goal oriented. Most of all, a disciplined person is selfless. The needs of others take precedence over his selfish desires. Without self-discipline, a rider cannot gain the horse's confidence, and so the guide will fail to guide him. Successful communication between two living things, regardless of their species, is based on full attention to one another. The horse's focus on the rider is based on trust. In order to school a horse, the rider must gradually replace the horse's instincts with his own guidance. Without entrusting his very life to our safekeeping, the horse cannot let go of his instinctive alertness to scan his environment for dangers. He must replace those instincts with acquired and educated attention to his rider.

In life, just as in riding, one ought to have goals. We set goals fully aware that we may never reach them. However, without setting them and charting a plan for their attainment, we have nothing to guide us. The greatest benefit of goal orientation is the seeming contradiction of having a goal that we can deviate from. Altering goals should not be whimsical, left to chance or based on mood. Emotional restlessness is not a good adviser. Goal orientation and goal alteration should be based on assessment of realities, refined by analysis to simpler terms.

A scattered mind, an inconsistent personality, a fragmented attention span, cannot bear fruit in horsemanship. The art of life and the art of riding are similar because both depend on focusing the mind on perception, awareness, and discovery.

Correct discovery depends on understanding that right and wrong are relevant concepts defined from the horse's point of view. Only that which benefits the horse is right and all that damages or destroys the horse is wrong. Therefore, the horse *verifies the quality and integrity* of the rider's work. Giving aids denotes helping.

Riding as a Dynamic

Few, if any, activities lend themselves to both usefulness and pleasure more than riding. Since riding involves the body, mind, and spirit, its thrills give satisfaction to riders in each of these three dimensions.

One of the great thrills for riders finds its source in the horse's compulsion to manifest his "emotions" instantly by physical changes. His fears, anger, confusion, caution, display of threat, readiness to attack, or take flight, will all be instantly obvious in his body: his posture, muscle tone, direction, speed, and energy of motion. Ever changing, each horse is different, each day, each hour, and each moment. Few activities are as full of surprises as riding. Nothing can be less predictable than a horse. The horse is totally integrated in body, mind, and spirit and, therefore, instantly acts out his feelings.

Equal to the thrills of feeling the physical changes caused by the feelings of horses is the unique human ability of the rider to camouflage, cover up and hide all his emotion by not displaying any physical changes. The disciplined adult (as a good rider must be) can and must hide his emotion from the horse and the observing public. The thrill of rewarding a horse while angry, or soothing a horse while in fear, the

FIGURE 1.3 *A wonderful half pass left at the trot viewed from behind shows the most important elements of this gymnastic movement: the horse's legs work with precise unity of impact on the ground by working in synchronized diagonal pairs. The outside hind leg of the horse is straddling, well-engaged, accepting the laterally displaced weight. The left hind and right front diagonal pair assumes precise weight-bearing, and ensure that suspension is well-maintained. Bending to the left and a relaxed posture prove that maximum engagement is achieved.*

rider experiences the thrills of "stiff upper lip" self-controls that come by controlling and hiding the physical displays of strongly felt emotion.

Disciplined human nature, and the ability to abstract, allows the rider to physically shield the horse from the rider's emotions. In fact, a rider ought to ride with controlled emotion and discipline, and never let anger, impatience, and frustration cause him to apply physical misuse of seat, legs, or hands. The thrill earned by the rider is one of being aware of his own victory in self-discipline, by succeeding in not communicating his emotional state to the horse by any physical manifestation. The skill of camouflaging emotion is uniquely human and remains at the heart of good horsemanship. If a rider cannot rise above his emotions, but displays them outwardly, physically, he will have sunk to the level of the animal world. And, while the horse's emotional display through physical manifestation is a source of thrills, the same display by the rider is a source of shame.

By mastering his emotional state, the rider, in fact, invites the additional thrill of better understanding of the horse's world. Personal emotional control, through self-discipline, liberates the rider to pay undivided attention to the horse's condition.

We never reach our goals in riding. Riding is like shooting at a moving target, and if, and when, we hit the bull's-eye, the thrills are incredible. The art of riding is based on the talent to continuously mix and blend activities, much as a painter mixes colors to paint an image. There is no simple hue and no end to the complexities of color blending possibilities in the riding art. The thrill is to arrive at the right mixture on a scale continuum from simplicity to complexity. The rider mixes and blends each movement of the horse with the right amount of collection, suspension, suppleness, elasticity, amplification of energy, and suspension until grand beauty is born. Even if it were to last only a brief moment, that is justification enough.

Riding is controlled transportation. The horse transmits his energy of locomotion to the rider who not only feels its power, direction, and speed but assumes, depending on his skills, more or less control of this wondrous energy. The horse's power is thrilling because its source is living, willful, individualistic, capricious, haughty, and instinct triggered. The horse is full of surprises, yet willing to submit to a greater or lesser extent to the rider's commanding authority. The controlling of the horse's energy, being neither in source nor in its controls mechanical, depends on the feel of the rider, his riding skills, his academic insight, and spiritual finesse. These are riding thrills unparalleled by challenges of mechanical transportation.

The sensation of blended unity of motion and participation in locomotion with another living creature brings its own excitement. Riding is related to dancing but can, indeed, be even more harmonious to an extent of sensing no demarcation between the two living organisms so intent on the unity of their balance, the firmness of their center of gravity, in seamless blended motion. Motion acclaimed by the unity of horse and rider can be much more varied than anything in dancing and is certainly faster, more powerfully sweeping, and overwhelming than dancing. The sensation of harmonious locomotion with an other than human creature adds to the thrills produced by both its harmony and its command. Intriguing is the unity and harmony in horsemanship that comes from human control of posture and locomotion, yet this control is made possible by the very energy in locomotion surrendered by the horse which it aims to command.

Even more thrilling to the rider is the sensation that while in enormously energetic motion and suspension, both he and the horse maintain a posture of isometric firmness, not unlike statuesque tranquility and poise, while continuing motion in unhindered fluidity. Both horse and rider must sensitively move and oscillate to accommodate each one of the participant's seemingly perfect balance at the very rate of movement required by the powerful thrust of locomotion. This postural tranquility, superb in tone yet lacking any tension, sweeping over the rider with a blanketing sensation of unity-born immobility, is maintained through sensational flight.

The thrills of flight go beyond the sense of speed. While riding, the sensation of flight is heightened by the sensation of weightlessness. Mankind has dreamed of flying like a bird, free in the elements, floating and weightless. The skilled rider's rewards include the ability to unite, with precision, his center of gravity with that of his horse, so that the resulting unity of motion creates the illusion of weightlessness in flight.

Riding includes intellectual challenges and emotionally heightened states simply because riding is a discovery tour. We perpetually visit unknown territory, deal with surprises, speculate on the unpredictable, and discover that predictions are inexact and that we must improvise.

Riding as a Baroque Art

During the sixteenth, seventeen and eighteen centuries great advances were made in scientific inventions and discoveries. The seventeenth and eighteenth centuries were referred to as the *Age of Enlightenment* also known as the *Age of Reason* or simply the *Enlightenment*. Facts mattered and needed to be verified before being accepted. At that time, people discerned that they could take responsibility for "improving" on nature by taming and grooming it. Humankind accepted responsibility for the improvement of nature through selective breading, grooming, taming, training, and even culturing it, thus potentially elevating random nature to the level of art. The natural horse is magnificent because its evolved form is efficient and unique. However, its behavior is random and unpredictable. Random nature, when altered by human intelligence and systems, could perform greater feats with less effort. Sophistication that nature would not volunteer is induced to perform as art. Human design and intelligence guided by rationally guided ideals could be used to alter nature's behavior, and through this transformative process, potentially become art. Sophistication that nature would not volunteer is induced to perform as art. The schooling of horses aims to bequeath him greater strength to carry his rider without undue stress on his mind and body.

The Age of Enlightenment held that human intelligence, and rational understanding were based on the truth of Rene Descartes' enlightened insight summed up by him as *"cogito ergo sum"* (I think, therefore I am). Nature cannot think. Therefore it falls to human consciousness to improve and elevate and groom the random products of nature. Sophistication that nature would not volunteer is induced by insights of human culture.

Most of our Equestrian Ideologies reflect the understandings gained during the baroque *Age of Reason*.

These pragmatic baroque principles regarding the art of riding and the taming and training of the horse are now scientifically mostly confirmed to be correct.

Through selective breeding programs animal species have been improved, and increased variants of species have resulted. From an artistic point of view, the fine art of riding was uniquely suitable for baroque stylization and expression because it was a "curvilinear" style of art where motion and exuberance are expressed in richly swirling, complex, overly decorated ways.

The triumph of baroque ideology is in creating an ennobled horse, which in turn raises his human partner to be both the object and the subject of a great art. Most of today's guiding principles in Classical riding came to us from the baroque centuries. Only in jumping horses were important discoveries added to the training traditions of the baroque age. The forward seat since 1911 has been successfully adapted for its great pragmatic value.

The triumph of baroque ideology created an ennobled horse, which in turn is so profoundly tamed, strengthened and given skills that now raises his human partner to be both the object and the subject of a great art.

The *equestrian arts* are baroque arts based on the principles of *enlightenment* and *reason*.

The baroque principle advocates that random nature could be transmuting to advanced art.

The horse is a magnificent creature of nature. He is efficient and unique. As all nature, the horse is random and unpredictable in his behavior.

During the Age of Reason scientific attitudes developed and, by reasoning, the baroque principle was born. Essentially, it advocated that rational humans can and often should improve on nature by grooming and altering it in service of a greater good. Most often inspired by aesthetic longing, making nature more orderly, predictable and organized was perceived as a human assignment. Intellect and aesthetic motivated and offered rational guidelines for the improvement on nature. By taming and grooming nature, one may improve on it and by organized intellect nature can become art. Random nature altered by human intelligence can make nature perform greater feats with less effort. Human design and intelligence guided by enlightened ideologies alters nature's behavior. Sophistication of baroque thinking believed that what nature would not volunteer to become can be, and even should be, induced by human intellect.

FIGURE 1.4 *This monument shows a horse with his tamer at the Palais Belvedere in Vienna, built for Prince Eugene of Savoy. It accurately represents the essentially baroque nature of horsemanship. Indeed, the greatest amount of riding knowledge was generated during the baroque culture by insight, innovation, experimentation, and standardization. Riding can truly be called a baroque art. At that time, the fundamental ideology accepted was that nature could be elevated to become art by taming, training, pruning, trimming, shaping, ordering, organizing, and cultivating. Mankind understood that nature is beautiful, though fierce and savage until man's intellect and genius of spirit elevates it by taming and ennobling it. The raw material of nature can only fulfill its potential when man's genius transforms it. Introducing order is essential to nature's intimate relationship with mankind, and this relationship remains noble and uplifting because it respects nature, never abuses or exploits it. It is only because of their admiration for nature that baroque men were inspired to order and cultivate it. They meant to elevate, not destroy—to fulfill, rather than spoil nature's potential.*

Through academic preparedness human intellect had been put to service in making horses lives totally free of pain, discomfort and damage by carrying the weight of a rider. Horses in nature are self-sufficient. However, horses bearing an unwelcome burden of a human need to be knowledgeably, systematically and gradually evolved to the "cultured" horse that by improved athletic posture and well-nurtured skills can evolve its strength to bear the burden of his rider without damage.

The horse, guided by an academically informed rider will learn to use his natural gifts with more efficiency, thereby promoting his useful life.

Most of our equestrian ideologies reflect the understandings gained by the baroque Age of Reason.

These pragmatic baroque principles are now scientifically confirmed to be correct. Baroque training goals are guided by devotion to the horse's well being. And while the rider caters to his horses' needs, so do the horses repay him by fostering the character improvement in riders and stimulate the evolution of human virtues.

The triumph of baroque ideology is in creating an ennobled horse, working with maximum efficiency through the humanly guided skills that allow large improvements in his strength. The baroque principle's triumph is manifested by mutual improvements between horse and rider. The horse gains joy in the ease of performing better with less effort as his effort is supplemented by skills and strength. As the horse is progressing in tameness, so is his rider improving on his virtues. Trust between them sets the horse free from be bondage of genetically coded compulsive behavior in exchange to trustful earned submission and obedience. Through this process of rational guidance and obedient submission the art of training horses, the human partner becomes the artist who creates the art by participating in it.

Chapter 2
The Classical Tradition

The classical riding tradition that has prevailed originated over three hundred years ago in France.

Because of that, we could argue that we ride according to the *French tradition*. We must remember, however, that all arts are dynamic and practitioners of them will alter the inherited concepts and practices according to their insights.

The origins of modern dressage practices can be found in the writings of the count François Robichon de la Guérinière, whose book, *Ecole de Cavalerie*, was published in 1733 [Xenophon Press 2015] and was inspired by the teachings of another French riding master, Antoine de Pluvinel [*The Manege Royal*, Xenophon Press 2015]. *Ecole de Cavalerie* became the equestrian bible, and the foundation of classical dressage as we know it today. De la Guérinière also invented or discovered the shoulder-in, one of the most highly valued suppling exercises we use today. He also taught us to ride with a leg position that promotes a perpetually draped leg contact with the horse. This leg position is based on shortening the stirrups to increase the flexion angles of the rider's joints, which, in turn, promote the right muscular flexion and isometric tone necessary for the engagement of the horse's hindquarters.

Riding institutions entrenched in the classical riding traditions such as the Spanish Riding School of Vienna and academies of the Hungarian riding tradition (the Spanish Riding School of Buda during the years 1922 to 1945 and Orkeney) followed the teachings of de la Guérinière (figs. 2.1 and 2.2). All the riders, trainers, and authors who have followed these institutional traditions maintained in the remains of the dismembered Habsburg Empire, are indebted to de la Guérinière for their ideologies, riding principles, and skills. In that sense, most thoughts, written and revered since, including great contributions by Germans, are footnotes to de la Guérinière.

I am not a believer in dividing classical equitation and training principles into "German" and "French" schools of dressage. There is only good riding and bad riding. No nation can claim to be the exclusive home of either. Labeling various riding styles or training methods seems to be speculative invention rather than tangible reality. I am unsettled and discouraged when I hear talk about splitting dressage along national lines. I still continue to stubbornly believe that all good riders are like-minded. They form a group that transcends national or cultural boundaries. Good riders constitute a supra-national community and are the custodians of the *enduringly effective and classical equestrian culture*. People who discern vast differences among national riding styles should notice instead, the redeeming similarities of ideologies and training methods among those who ride and train well. Indeed, good equestrians represent a cohesive and comprehensible culture that is not defined by national boundaries. The

FIG 2.1

FIG 2.2

FIGURES 2.1 AND 2.2 *Geza Hazslinszky-Krull was a demigod to me in my teen years. He was one of the most beautiful riders I have ever seen on a horse—a monument of perfection in seat and aids. As is always the case with great riders, the art comes from within. This man's legendary goodness, refinement, "politesse," and diplomatic elegance gave pleasure to all around him. He was one of those great gentlemen, who as a "species" seems to have vanished today. We all glowed in his presence. He was terribly soft-spoken to both his horses and to his students. He has the seat to emulate, including the "toes up," a phrase he never tired of whispering during lessons. In the first photo, note the horse's spirit, not to mention his joyous dancing in gravity-defying splendor.*

equestrian culture, with its own distinct traditions, vocabulary, conceptual certainties, and strong advocacy of right from wrong, remains international.

There could, however, be a legitimate perception of difference in riding traditions along national or regional lines due to peculiarities arising in the schooling of different breeds of horses. While the concepts of lightness of aids and of obvious self-carriage of horses must be identical beyond national boundaries, the specific translation of these concepts into riding realities will differ when a rider presents these concepts on different breeds. An Iberian, a French Anglo-Arabian, or a German Hanoverian will react and respond differently to riding influences. Highly varied in temperament, conformation, and physical strength, these horses will need the application of differing degrees of aids. For that matter, each horse is, in fact, an individual, and warrants variable riding skills. Therefore, I think, that when observing performances on a superficial level, some might appear "lighter," while others seem to be the result of "hard work." Similarly, depending on an observer's education, discerning collection on a lighter, more *petite* horse might look very different from collection on an equine giant. Yet, to educated eyes and principled minds these concepts can be discerned easily without compartmentalizing them into French or German schools of riding.

This is the very reason why I mourn the disappearance of great riding institutions, where one was compelled to ride hundreds of different horses, yet we owned none of them. We learned to ride the "species horse" and not a "dear one."

The Iberian horse breeds—including the Lipizzan, the Andalusian, and the Lusitano—tend to be small and agile, exquisitely balanced, with powerful haunches, short and strong backs, and supporting a tall carriage of well-arching necks. Such conformational features may render them especially suitable for collected movements such as the piaffe and passage and even for the remarkable airs above the ground. They easily crouch down, tuck their lumbar back and thrust their pelvis forward, allowing them to raise their forehand like a crane lifting freight off the ground. Such a configuration can be seen with every horse performing the *levade*.

However, in the nineteenth century, riding needs and consequently styles, changed. Three-day eventing, fox hunting, cross-country riding, and jumping became enormously popular. As a result, people wanted horses that were more versatile and more ground-gaining in stride than were horses bred primarily for *manège* work and collection. Ground-gaining gaits and speed grew in popularity while dressage schooling retained its overpowering significance as the only truly therapeutic riding tradition that enhanced the horse's useful and serviceable years. Dressage was viewed as the proper means to the diverse ends sought by riders. At about the middle of the eighteen century, Germany became the first country to establish a specific breeding program for the development of "sport horses" in order to supply the demand for something different from the baroque horse. Since then, as a result of nearly three hundred years of dedication, expertise, and performance testing, the various European warmbloods have succeeded in producing "super horses" that can amplify the basic gaits so sensationally as never seen before. Born with grand and supple gaits, these horses are monuments to genetic engineering and selective breeding, and give contemporary riders possibilities our forebears never had.

There should be no difference between classical and competitive riding when competitors are pursuing the right training goals. Competition is designed to show excellence in classical schooling of horses. The purpose of dressage competition is the showing of exemplary training triumphant in a supple, collected, engaged, and contented horse. Riders compete for the approximation of ideals that were established centuries ago and should be scored according to this approximation of ideals. In fact, the F.E.I. (The International Equestrian Federation) is the guardian of classical riding principles, and simultaneously the supervisor and administrator of the highest levels of competitions. To that end, the F.E.I. also reserves the right to accredit the judges acceptable for judging at international dressage events. Therefore, we should expect the F.E.I. to promote classical schooling by rewarding riders representing that schooling.

There is no mystery to classical equitation. It is the pragmatic tradition of riding in which correct content defines the correct form (style). It is an enduring equestrian tradition precisely because it is pragmatic. It endorses the principles of riding that prolong the useful life of most horses, most of the time. It is kind and therapeutic riding with the goal of making life comfortable for the horse under his rider and for the rider seated on his horse. All concepts, such as physical suppleness and elasticity or mental focus, attention, and obedience, are subsidiary to that primary goal.

Custodians of the Classical Tradition

The standards of all living arts are maintained by the degree of excellence shown in their practice. Riding is a living art and survives only to the extent it is practiced correctly by those who represent it.

Riders die ignorant. The more we study and practice any art, the more we recognize our ignorance of it. Therein resides the lesson of humility. Riders become aware of the inexhaustible nature of equestrian knowledge and that knowledge hinges on discovering living individuals, discerning their needs and wants and administering

FIGURE 2.3 *By using a photograph of Colonel Josipovich, I am paying tribute to the great equestrian heritage that resided in the Austro-Hungarian Empire. When Hungary became autonomous after the First World War, the uniformity and correctness of equestrian arts was in the custody of one of Europe's greatest riding academies, Orkenytabor. One of its most notable directors was Zsigmond Josipovich, who was followed by the well-known names of Waldemar Seunig* (Horsemanship: A Comprehensive Book on Training the Horse and Its Rider) *and Lt. Col. Agoston d'Endrödy* (Give Your Horse a Chance).

to them to the best of our ability. All of these elements are intangible, inexhaustible, difficult to validate, and ever-changing. Most art is dynamic. The equestrian arts are among the most dynamic.

An eminent student of Josipovich was one of my four great teachers, Dr. Jeno Reznek. Along with the others, Dr. Pal Kemery, Imre Bodo, and Geza Hazslinszky-Krull, they all became eminent teachers at the Orkenytabor Academy. Based on exchange programs for outstanding equestrian educators, all these teachers of mine attended two additional foreign riding academies, at Tor di Quinto or Pinerolo in Italy, Wienerneustadt or Vienna in Austria, or Hannover in Germany. They were distinguished international competitors—their knowledge influenced by their travels yet standardized by the classical tradition.

Notice the impeccable seat, the tall, toned, composed posture of tranquility, the flexed ankles into short enough stirrups to allow the knees to close, and the calf to stretch. The stability of his hands is obvious, resulting from shoulders back-

and-down continuing into vertical, therefore weightless, hanging upper arms. His elbows motionlessly define the vertical seat, which allows the horse's bridle to be steadily presented.]

There are, of course, custodians of the equestrian arts today. Few riders, however, are sophisticated or knowledgeable enough to discern who really knows the teachings and the heritage of the classical riding tradition. Even the choice of mentors, teaching and coaching masters, requires some level of expertise. Sometimes ignorant riders, unqualified to instruct, become self-appointed representatives of the equestrian culture, of which they are barely aware.

Good riding should be the "calling card" of an equestrian expert, yet good riding must not be confused with showing successfully. Scoring well, during a somewhat subjective method of evaluation and under special circumstances that may last for a mere six to twelve minutes, is not an adequate documentation of expertise.

In the classical tradition of horsemanship, respect for riders is allotted in accordance with their inborn riding abilities and their acquired riding skills. Traditionally, respect was allotted to riders proportionate to their riding wisdom and their understanding of each horse. The art of riding is correct equitation.

Good horsemanship includes more than skilled riding. Significantly, it includes familiarity with the equestrian tradition as well as remaining a participant in the current evolutionary process of an age-old equestrian tradition.

Wherever I have traveled, on four continents, riders complain that their equitation is seldom corrected and their riding skills are rarely tutored. In fact, the improvement of their riding skills is often ignored. Instead, lessons frequently concentrate on "teaching the horse" regardless of the inefficiencies of a rider lacking skills. An improperly sitting rider who gives the aids poorly cannot improve just by being on the horse, regardless of how many times school "figures and patterns" are repeated. In riding, there is no neutrality. We either habituate improvement or habituate disaster. Habituation of riding mistakes and performance mistakes are not legitimate teaching goals.

We need to improve ourselves as riders *before* we can improve our horses. That is precisely why we give riding lessons and not "*horsing* lessons." Coaching complex school movements, such as flying changes or half-passes with riders lacking the skills to "aid = help" their horses perform them, is not correct teaching. It merely demonstrates ignorance of the subject matter.

Riders are often to blame for receiving inappropriate instruction. They coerce teachers into coaching beyond their knowledge level by threatening to withdrawing their patronage.

One of the threats to the classical tradition of equestrian arts is caused by the fact that riders are also paying customers, clients, of the instructors. They can subtly or overtly dictate "the merchandise" that they are willing to pay for. Not being experts themselves, they are not good arbiters of the "merchandise." Because they are customers and "consumers" of lessons, many riders guide, if not determine, the instructor's teaching priorities.

In sharp contrast to these contemporary threats to correct teacher/pupil relationships stand the examples from the past. Formerly, equestrian education was in the curriculum of military academies. In these riding academies, teachers did not need to cater to the whims of a paying clientele, nor were teachers instructed by students as to their wishes and purported needs. Students had to learn enough riding skills to survive the tedium of parades and the rigors of the battlefield. Both were matters of survival. Riders with more talent and ambition than the average recruit became riding masters, responsible for the education of future generations of horses and riders. They did not avail themselves of a privileged equestrian education by paying for it. They were chosen, selected, honored by the experts at riding academies who invited them to stay for a course. The riders were selected by their teachers. Not the other way around, as it is done today. It was a meritocracy.

Ignorant and vain customers may well be profitable. They are welcomed because they supply the economic support for the continued survival of the equestrian arts and the promotion of the equestrian culture. Notwithstanding, some riders under continuous, consistent and frequent tutoring often receive excellent instruction. Their instructor must face their shortcomings frequently enough to serve as a motivational force for the eventual elimination of bad habits. Frequent and regular interaction between student and teacher facilitates elimination of equitation faults. In sharp contrast, in a clinic system of instruction, teachers, and students interact infrequently and then only for short periods, which encourages tolerance for bad riding and equitation. Both the instructor and the students are assured of the brevity of their mutual irritation.

Every person, when riding, reveals his inner self. Facial expressions, body posture, manners toward the horse, attitude toward the task at hand, allow us to read the rider like an open book. When riding a horse, we cannot hide easily from the perceptions of an informed observer. If we accept that elegance is the result of doing anything well without being self-conscious about it, then elegant riding is the culmination of the equestrian's art. Elegance is unaffected, effortless exquisiteness. Teaching *to attain elegance*, instead of *collecting high scores in competitions*, should be the task of equestrian professionals.

Great teachers inspire because they have knowledge of their craft and the moral courage to uphold its highest standards (fig. 2.3). My hope is that the riding public will change its market demands from vanity-oriented coaching to an uncompromising desire for impeccable equitation.

Chapter 3
Classical versus Competitive Riding

In contemporary competitions, the movements that test the horse's proper gymnastic evolution toward fulfillment of his genetic potential is proceeding on a grand scale. Contemporary competition requires of horses great competency in "gymnastic vocabulary." In comparing past performances required of well-schooled horses, the "keyboard" for riding has been extended many octaves. From the highest degree of collection to the longest extension, the contemporary "super horse" is asked to display an athletic vocabulary unmatched in the past for its versatility, power, and elegance.

Those who claim that deviation from the classical training principles and riding norms is necessary to be competitive do not seem to understand the goals of equitation.

There is only one correct way of riding: *riding for the good of the horse and not for the expectations of judges*. Riding is to benefit horses, not to please any judges. However, and not coincidentally, when a judge knows his science and commands the necessary crafts and skills, he will recognize in the horse the physical and mental manifestations that document how well he was schooled for his own sake. Expert judges appreciate riding that benefits the horse and such riding will please the onlooker (as it should) including the judge. There is only one knowledgeable, systematic, and gradual way of developing riders who can train horses with their well-being as the object of schooling. Therefore, competitive riding should be synonymous with classical riding simply because competitors are invited to show excellence in virtues as they are defined by the classical riding tradition. The goals of training and the means to achieve them should be well-known and shared by members of the equestrian culture. The rewards to have excelled in them ought to be predictable.

Classical riding is founded on the enduring principles of riding that represent the sum total of riding experience. Hundreds of generations through millions of riders over many centuries have explored horses and horsemanship. The cumulative wisdom derived from their experience is represented by the body of knowledge we call "classical horsemanship."

Competition should make classical principles victorious. When it does not, the reasons may be circumstantial. The breeders who produce the "super horses" that can perform without principled, knowledgeable, and respectable riders, top the list of those to whom "credit is due" for competition victories by horses without the benefit of good schooling. Ineptitude, poor showmanship, accidental omission of details, and trivial mistakes can influence the outcome of competitions.

Most importantly, judges represent a varied range of expertise. They may be also be influenced by additional factors: fatigue, the inability to focus, and a lack of dedication to the task at hand.

FIGURE 3.0 *Competition success indeed rewards correct training. Observe the horse on the aids displaying the poll as the highest point of his posture. Great thrust of energy from lowered haunches elevates the whither and the left forehand to a vertical canon bone. The clarity of correct weight distribution is obvious as the left hind and right forehand are in perfect synchrony supporting the weight the left forehand is lifted twice as high as the right hind. All of this correct vision includes a relaxed, pleased horse with skillfully accommodating the rider's aids.*

Even under the best of circumstances, the very best judges must weigh and consider a great number of factors on which to base their judgment and assign their scores. Scores are due within seconds of the pragmatically and impartially observed events. The volatility of circumstances at the show grounds, the great range and variety of talent in horses showing, and the variety in personality, as well as a variation in the expertise of judges, will all influence the outcome of competitions. Therefore, the ranking of riders may not precisely reflect the excellence in schooling, not because of malice or occasional weakness of expertise by the judges but because the other, highly variable, circumstances in the performance may have favored a less deserving rider with higher scores.

In the brief history of competitive dressage riding that began in the last decades of the nineteenth century, I am not aware of any epoch that did not suffer occasionally from poor judgment by some judges. Riders were rarely satisfied and the expectations of all competitors were never met. A prominent judge, who I greatly respected, used to say that at the end of every dressage class there is surely one very pleased rider: the winner. And, he advised dejected riders to cheer up because if they ride well and consistently for a long time, they will eventually be recognized and rewarded by judges.

Competition can be a rewarding exercise for goal orientation and discipline. It can be an excellent opportunity for seeking expert evaluation, guidance, and enlightened comments. It can be a great learning experience. Competition sharpens riders by focusing them on improved equitation and by making them aware that they are public performers.

We must acknowledge that judges cannot be equally expert or equally well suited by personality for the skills needed for rapid and accurate judgment. Often they cling to one or two easily recognizable features in the horse, such as a certain posture or tempo, and use one or two selected features by which they judge. Their entire evaluative procedure could be based on simple, easily recognizable equestrian "mantras," without proper understanding of the larger, legitimate gymnastic goals of training. They establish a scale of virtues and vices based on the degree of display of the few features they find recognizable and can monitor. These, certainly for them, become very important. Other elements in the rider's presentation go unrecognized and are deemed unimportant, incidental, trivial.

Riders often complain that they had to ride according to the discovered mantras of a particular judge in order to gain praise and placement. At times, when the fashion called for a high and confined neck carriage pulled up and together by harsh hands and exhausting contact, it was justified by calling for the classical principle demanding that the poll be the highest point of the horse. Then one could see inverted horses win. Of course every horse that is moving "above the bit" in an inverted position, using the sympathetic muscle system suitable for fighting and resistance, was escaping the rider's influences. By this posture the horse's hindquarters remained disengaged, his balance and gaits destroyed. But his poll was carried at the highest point. So if that is all the judge can recognize, whether it is a poll carried high due to well-engaged haunches or carried high due to inversion, the standard for evaluating schooling becomes singular and dangerous. From such judgments riders become confused, misguided and begin to feel that the classical schooling of a horse is not recognized and rewarded in the show ring.

Equally confusing to riders presenting supple, collected, elastic, and engaged horses is the occasional dissatisfaction of certain judges with their tempo. Sometimes judges criticize them for being "slow, inactive, lazy and lacking impulsion." These critical comments incite riders to run their horses off their feet. The sad picture presented is a running horse as if pulling an invisible buggy. The carriage horse should indeed run as fast as his legs can shuffle because his burden is pulled behind him and need not be lifted. The riding horse, however, ought to be trained to move with great animation by the increased articulation of his joints (impulsion) but without increasing speed, for he needs to lift and carry. Hence, the eternal importance of half-halting for the purpose of rebalancing horses toward their haunches (collection) and increasing their activity yet decreasing their speed (engagement of the quarters). The results of haste and rushing include the destruction of balance, the diminishing of length of strides and loss of flexibility in the joints and a destruction of the gaits. When judges demand rushing and haste in the name of promoting "impulsion" they show a misunderstanding of what impulsion is and a disregard for the horse's development in

FIGURE 3.1 *The powerful transition from collected to medium canter is a wonderful presentation of extending the stride length without rushing or rapidity of rhythm. Lowering of the croup allows the horse to work deeply under and to remain in increased impulsion. Long strides triumph with withers rising while the croup lowers. This is a visual example of my saying: "legs energize, seat modifies, reins verify." Engagement is triumphant by not losing the haunches as more weight-bearing by haunches demon- strate the "mystery" of a horse maintaining collection even during extension. The horse has developed the appropriate strength and skills to execute an extension without losing "collection!" Beautiful posture verifies the correctness of the work.*

unity toward collection and suppleness. They promote the development of horses that become movers of their limbs without body participation. That is the opposite of the goals of dressage.

Those who understand classical schooling know that both *speed and inversion*—along with *crookedness*—are the *escape mechanisms* of horses that refuse to submit their haunches to their rider. Judges who encourage schooling the skills by which horses escape from their riders, namely *speed, inversion* and *crookedness*, do a disservice to the promotion and upholding of classical training goals. One needs only to recall the majesty of the passage and the localization of the piaffe to know that the epitome of classical schooling is displayed without haste. No amount of haste can hurry riders to their slow majesty. Nor do we need to look further than the Spanish Riding School where horses cantering, trotting, and passaging are accompanied on the ground by slow-striding attendants. Ask yourself what would happen to you if you walked along the side of a cantering horse. You would be left behind. That is a sure sign of lack of collection, engagement, and most of all, a total lack of impulsion.

Working on the long rein, a horse must perform in all gaits without rushing his handler guiding him from the ground. All school movements are performed during long reining at a tempo not exceeding the walking pace of the person on the ground.

To misguide riders and confuse them by demanding haste, speed, inversion, tension and so on, will confuse them and bring to their mind the inevitable conclusion that there is a rupture, an irreconcilable difference, between classical schooling and competitive success. That is a tragedy.

Once ignorant judging causes trainers to pursue incorrect goals through incorrect means, they, in turn, will start to encourage the same in their pupils in order to keep their clientele competitively successful. This is especially important in an equestrian society where there are few who can discern good riding, and where competition ranking has become the standard measurement for riding prestige and credibility.

From the judges, ideas flow to trainers and coaches and from them, ideas are passed to their riders. A few ill-informed people with judging authority can cause many trainers to comply with them and, in turn, misguide, hundreds of riders. From the capstone of this pyramid, down to its vast base, a disaster may result.

Conversely, if the custodians of classical equitation are expert judges, they will encourage the best tendencies in trainers and coaches, and the riding public will find that their classical equitation and their properly schooled supple horses will win praise and high scores. If such is the case, the re-convergence of classical riding with competition will be insured and obvious to all participants in the art of riding. To succeed in this effort, one needs well-educated equestrian societies with an equestrian culture shared by all participants, regardless of their talent or riding level. Judges, teachers, and riders should understand the same concepts, principles and pursue them diligently. Cultural unity in pursuit of any art depends on a shared understanding of the definitions of the major concepts, aspirations, and goals involved.

The True Meaning of Winning

I believe that the rider who brings out the best gymnastic development of a meager horse is winning his own Olympic Gold medal based on exactly the same criteria as the actual winner of an Olympic Gold. For they both honor the horse's talents in a kindly manner. The Olympic winner, however, has one of the best horses. While another fine rider on a horse with scanty inherited resources still may erect an enduring private monument to good horsemanship, while the Olympic winner is deservedly, publicly monumentalized.

The competition tests do not, by themselves, promote incorrect training; people do. What contact or impulsion or self-carriage or collection mean and should mean are often misunderstood. Because we have broken the continuum of education offered by credible riding academies, we are seeing the breaking down—but we hope not the end—of an equestrian culture. All the participants in a "culture"

---

[1] A technical term, a term of art.

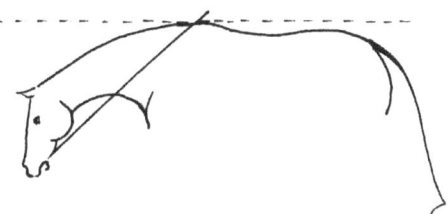

FIGURE 3.2 *The result of giving hands: the correctly stretched horse, now a required activity in some competition tests, stretches his neck forward and then sinks it down in its entirety below the withers. This is also the correct posture for the "long-and-low" positioning of the neck for training purposes.*

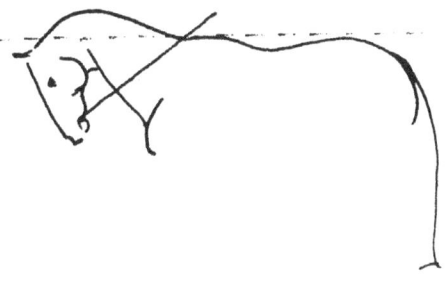

FIGURE 3.3 *Roll Kur is the result of confining hands: in sharp contrast to the above is an incorrect procedure to lower the poll where the neck is forced to rise on a braced lower neck muscle into a "cobra neck." It is then "broken" abruptly at the third or fifth vertebra, dropping the face behind the verti- cal, and confining the chin toward the chest.*

understand its *terminus technicus*[1] much like in the medical or legal professions where words and concepts need not be explained because their practitioners received an identical education. Members of the current equestrian culture come from vastly different backgrounds and represent the results of diverse "educational levels" and proficiencies. Competition tests are not at fault when performances are contrary to good horsemanship.

Correctly schooled horses are always light. They need not belong to a special national school or riding style. This is because when a rider correctly presents the bit to his horse, the bit will represent the rider's seat and the horse will stretch through his top-line to contact the bit but not the rider's hands. And, the contact will not be with the horse's mouth but with his hocks.

The horse's mouth will be closed, his neck arched with liquid (not braced) muscles. His head will hang loosely from his poll and he will feel light to the rider who will sense a lack of stress, an emptiness in his hands and arms, feeling merely the weight of the reins in his hands. Contact is the connection of the horse's hocks to the bridle, achieved by stepping through a rounded and elevated back, and a loosely hanging neck, which allows the horse to feel the termination of this energy from the haunches, on the bit (fig. 3.2). The half-halt is used as a repeated reminder to the horse to collect his center of gravity back toward his haunches and then the hocks, which are his springing, sprinting, lifting joints.

Without lightness that produces self-carriage, riders cannot control the hindquarters of the horse. Were there stress and tension in the reins and hands, the horse would lean against them in desperation for freedom from their confining pressures. Horses inhibited, confined, and stiffened by hands and reins will eventually break down. Misguided riders want to produce an artificially set neck, their misunderstood icon of collection (fig. 3.3), but by those actions they cannot mobilize the horse's back from the soft transmission of the energy of well-engaged haunches. They forget that the horse has three "bascules," and the neck is merely the first to flex. The second bascule is the contraction of the abdominal muscles of the horse that allow elevation, loosening, and swinging of the back. The last bascule is the sophisticated rounding and lowering of the haunches. These gather under the rider for lifting and carrying. The horse sinks his croup and crouches closer to the ground on strengthened and supple joints that flex not only when lifting a limb but also when impacting on the ground. Eventually, on the F.E.I. level tests, the horse has to "sit" and lower his croup, flex at the lumbosacral joint, and sink on his joints toward the ground when he impacts on it. This is only possible by riding from hocks to bridle in self-carriage.

Many riders have an outstanding competition record precisely because they practice the principles of the classical training tradition. Examples of such riders include the late Dr. Reiner Klimke, Klaus Balkenhol, Arthur Kottas-Heldenberg, and Gyula Dallos (figs. 3.4 a & b).

As I mentioned earlier, there are many fine riders with their minds, hearts, and equitation in the right place. I have seen riders who are young and compete at lower levels; they are well schooled and talented. Many years ago, I proposed that those of us who teach and judge should create a database of riders we find exceptionally talented and with the right character, so that the riding community could assist them, through scholarships to study or clinic with greater teachers, to become the future professionals who will be the guardians of the classical tradition.

FIGURES 3.4 A & B *Gyula Dallos and Aktion, stars of many competitions, freestyles, and exhibition rides, received many standing ovations, earning their places in spectators' hearts. The stallion's posture always remains poised and noble, with neck muscles correctly flexed and developed to look thick and continuous like a quarter of a doughnut, arriving at his shoulder as those particular muscles should when they are correctly developed.*

FIG 3.4 A

FIG 3.4 B

Part 2:
Training the Horse

Chapter 4
The Nature of the Horse

The horse is part of nature. The purpose of nature is to promote its own survival. When any energy is expended, it is for the sake of the individual and the survival of the species. When survival is achieved, nature seeks inertia. Animals eat, watch out for predators, flee from danger, and reproduce in order to survive. If these activities were not necessary for their survival, they would prefer to take a nap. Nature takes it easy. Even rivers take the path of least resistance—downhill. Animals are genetically programmed, through the process of natural selection, to sustain the most efficient mixture of survival activity and inertia.

Humans cannot influence animals unless we attract their attention. Therefore, the extent to which we can influence our horses depends on how successful we are in getting them to focus on us. A rider gradually gains the horse's attention and should aim at extending the length of time he is able to sustain it. Eventually, when he can gain the horse's complete attention, he has gained his submission. Having attracted his attention and commanded his submission, he can gain control of the energy emitting from his haunches. By harnessing the horse's energy, he may direct it to produce the desired locomotion. To achieve control of the horse's haunches, a rider must possess the skill of connecting the horse's hocks through properly postured longitudinal flexion to the bridle. Having achieved flexion and having attracted the horse's attention, the rider's work will bear fruit in a supple horse that moves with amplified gaits, in reliable balance, and with more of his weight over his haunches. The resulting lightness of his forehand allows the horse a spectacular display of his gaits, floating, while his posture remains steady, proud, and tall with *hauteur*.

To surrender their entire attention to us is, for our horses, a most unnatural thing to do, and an utter compromise of their inherited genetic programming for the promotion of their survival. Lucky for us, horses are also genetically programmed to focus on something—anything—at all times. They continuously scan their surroundings and focus on whatever attracts their attention in order to determine whether it is a threat. Then they either take flight or continue to scan for the next object of fascination. A rider can redirect his horse's focus-mania through attention-getting communication that should be based on reward. In this way, in time, a horse's survival instincts can be replaced by total trust in his rider, who becomes his "partner in survival." The development of this partnership is at the heart of the process of taming horses.

Through a nurturing relationship with their riders, horses are tamed to learn an "artificial" behavior pattern, a "culture," that we impose on them. From then on, they live parallel lives, and can alternate between nature-coded and "cultured," or learned, behavior. By lapsing in and out of mental states of being, a horse can act as either a "natural" horse in a "pastoral" state of mind, or a "cultured" horse with a "schooled" mentality of submission to the human will.

When alone, a schooled horse reverts to nature's state of scanning to focus on threats. But when he is with his rider, whom he recognizes as his protector, his guide, his mentor, and the source of his pleasure, he focuses on his will. The rider becomes *nurture's* partner for survival as he replaces *nature's* codified instincts.

It is natural and instinctive for horses to become startled. Those horses that did not become startled are no longer with us, because they were eaten by predators. The horses that are with us today are here because their ancestors were good at being startled.

However, if the rider also gets startled (a learned and inexcusable fear-displaying behavior) when the horse does, then the horse will learn to shy. Shying is a learned and prolonged behavior. It is not genetically coded but rather is acquired—in other words, taught, schooled, and "cultured"—behavior. Horses on the range do not shy. In truth, horses shy but from one thing: work!

Timid riders and those who lose their focus when the horse redirects it, will cause— even manufacture—shying behavior.

Horses will shy with increasing frequency and intensity as lapses in the rider's control reoccur. The horse learns that when he reacts to external environmental stimuli, and redirects his rider's focus to them, the rider loses balance and control. This provides a horse with both a "rewarding" and a "punishing" experience, which encourages in him a worsening of his shying behavior.

Riders commonly, inadvertently reward their horses' startling by allowing rest periods from having to focus on the rider and from having to submit their haunches to work. Only the submission of the haunches allows the rider to control where, and in what manner, the horse will move. As the rider loses attention and with it, his control through the system of aids, the horse learns that he can get a "vacation" by feigning interest in his environment. As he points his ears and focuses his eyes on the object of his pretended caution, he inverts his bending, drifts his haunches away from the object of his "fascination," and finds that the rider has surrendered control. Great power is surrendered by the rider who permits shying because with it, comes the proof that the rider cannot control his transportation. Both the mind and the haunches of the horse escape the rider's control.

The most harmful lesson a horse learns is that his startled reaction or flight may cause his rider to hurt him, usually with hands jerking on his sensitive mouth or with spurs gripping his sides. An unpredictable rider's erratic actions may also trigger the horse's instinctive fear of falling. He may come to fear the rider's reaction more than the object, the event, or sound that initially attracted his attention. Eventually, he may learn to respond with fear of his rider as soon as a strong environmental stimulus appears. Not only will he notice sounds and sights, but will also overreact to them by bolting, shying, spinning, or rearing, because he expects each stimulus to be followed by a horrendous onslaught of punishment.

FIGURE 4.0 *The horse should always determine the carriage of his neck. Observing the actions of his limbs the horse demonstrates that he is uninhibited by the reins. By the freedom, reach and height in the use of his legs, the horse verifies his motion in self-carriage.*

Horses, then, can develop a "secondary" fear conditioned by inappropriate rider reaction, much in the way that Pavlov's dogs became conditioned to salivate at the sound of a ringing bell. In truth, many of the things that we think scare horses are not interesting to them, and in a natural environment would easily be ignored. However, the "nurture" of a bad rider alerts, alarms, and panics the horse into *unnatural* learned reactions.

Horses are, with good reason, suspicious of their riders as potential sources of pain. A timid rider, or one with a foul temper and a lack of self-control, easily confirms this suspicion. Should there be a "rider problem," the horse will remain watchful of objects that can provoke the rider's tumultuous behavior and result in the anticipated blows to the mouth, death-grip with the spurs to his sides, and an imbalanced rider that makes him anxious of falling. He will shy and take flight in order to flee the source of his hurt. Little does his rider suspect that the horse knows very well how to get rid of the source of his real—not the pretended—fears: the rider!

Riders who are ignorant of the ease with which horses can become increasingly prone to shying blame the behavior on environmental oddities and potential causes of spooking. They become unwitting partners to their horses' misbehavior. To such a rider, the horse will pretend that he has just had a vision, and became flabbergasted, thereby setting off the vicious circle produced by a horse afraid of his rider and a rider afraid of his horse. Phlegmatic horses are too inert to have "visions." They are reluctant to expend the energy to be startled. Instead, they point their ears, eyes, head and neck toward any object of interest, much as a guide on a tour bus will channel the attention of the passengers toward the sights. Horses train their riders to join their "sightseeing tours," and haphazardly swoon around taking thoughtful, extended looks at things not worth a gasp.

In effect, horses attempt to train their riders into becoming fellow travelers of their ilk, making us more like them—a high price to pay for an unpredictable coexistence on an out-of-balance progression through space. The smart partner will not relinquish control to the strong partner.

To halt the cycle begun with the natural startling of the young horse, a rider must remain "bored" with it, maintaining balance and lightening the rein contact to pretend partnership with his horse's natural instinct to flee. Far from inhibiting the flight impulse, the rider should participate in it for a few strides and then turn this flight energy into controlled locomotion and impulsion by actually driving the fleeing horse.

Flight energy is good energy if the rider recognizes the opportunities to transform it from potential energy into engagement. Light hands are indispensable for the building of confidence in the young horse, and trust in the more schooled one. After a horse is startled, the rider must drive him forward enthusiastically by increasing his tempo or by making an upward transition to a potentially faster gait. When this happens, the horse finds himself partnered in his flight instinct—yet also instantly controlled. Horses "live" in their haunches, not in their heads! Their awareness is motor-awareness; therefore, they submit when they are driven forward, not when they are confined or held back. "Reasoning" with a horse happens when the rider controls the haunches, the source of the horse's energy.

The rider should neither attempt to soothe a startled horse with voice nor confuse him by patting. Horses in flight do not need rewarding, but rather, a quick redirecting of their energy. Since horses cannot analyze, synthesize, and reason, they will only recognize the power of persuasion inherent in increased work with the haunches.

For a rider to stop a shying horse with a session of "show and tell" is counterproductive. A horse will not accept environmental phenomena either by being pushed toward it or by being made to face it in the hope of looking at it. That would solve nothing with an animal that cannot reason. Familiarity with sights has never stopped shying, only increased work solves shying. Making horses stare at meaningless objects reveals the common, yet irrational, rider attempt to "humanize" their mounts. A horse learns nothing by standing and facing something he has noticed, but instead, will prance and fidget in front of it in utter incomprehension or enjoy an unintended rest (reward) period.

A rider must command the horse's attention not only while in the saddle but also while on the ground. The rider must insist that the horse concentrate on him, replacing the horse's scanning for objects of interest by an unbroken attention to the rider (fig. 4.0).

We must deserve our horse's attention and respect. We cannot take it for granted. This develops through *acts of kindness and rewards. Slow in motion, soft in speech, and soothing in manner, the rider becomes a respected, reliable partner and a source of pleasure to the herd-bound horse.* Soon, his natural instincts for herd communication and perpetual focusing become "cultured" behavior through consistent, nurturing contact with humans. Remember that *dressage* is a French word that is accepted as the most accurate description of the concept of "taming for training" of a horse.

Correcting Escape Mechanisms and Evasions

Task reduction, minimizing effort, and *avoiding work* are at the top of the horse's agenda. The rider must realize that what the horse needs is often opposite from what the horse wants. The horse's needs are determined by the unnatural intrusion of the rider's weight on his back. The horse wants to retain the status quo of natural effortlessness. This includes his inborn crookedness and propensity to propel himself by pushing his center of gravity toward his structurally heavier forehand (head, neck, shoulder, and chest). In this manner, much of his ground gaining is achieved by kinetic energy, by falling forward after the initial push off. The horse progresses with minimal effort because the weight of his heavy forehand pulls him onward as if in a free fall of weight by gravitational forces, the way a person would fall down a staircase after an initial push.

In training horses, riders must observe the principle that what the horse *wants us to do* is often the opposite of what we *ought to do* to enable him to carry our foreign weight without mental or physical stress. The horse seeks a symbiotic relationship in which he inadvertently modifies his rider's behavior, position, balance, and posture to synchronize with and match his own. The horse's physical, gymnastic needs are most often opposite from his natural wants. Therefore, riding wisdom—data plus introspection resulting in understanding and insight—suggests that we always aim for what is for the good of the horse rather than become a partner to his shortcomings.

Any rider on the back of a horse must spend much of his effort apologizing to the horse for being there. Intelligence enhanced by education and experience, provide the ability to plan and institute changes that make the rider's apologies to the horse possible.

Horses try to evade their rider's influence by three major escape mechanisms based on their natural inclination to avoid working with the haunches. Horses find it easier to push rather than to lift and carry their rider. It is easier to shuffle with small steps and drag their feet on the ground. They try to avoid increased articulation of their joints and the reorganization of their balance that results from moving with a longitudinally flexed posture. Horses escape the rider's control over their haunches by the following major categories of evasions:

1. *Inversion* of the top-line—using their sympathetic muscle system for fighting or resistance. Variations include over-flexion and head tossing.

2. *Speeding up* the rhythm of their footfall, rushing their tempo by running on their forehand as rapidity necessitates progression by the body's weight pulling the structure forward with kinetic energy. Alternatively, horses can evade by lack of speed or by sluggishness, reluctance or refusal to go forward.

3. *Moving crookedly*—shoulders in or out relative to the line of progression of the hips, and haunches traveling in or out relative to the shoulder's progression. Crookedness can also result from their moving without spinal alignment. This produces un-level, uneven, choppy, stiff strides and a jarring motion that blocks the flow of energy from hocks to bridle and causes stress points in the body.

It is fascinating to recognize that these *three escape mechanisms* once adjusted, refined, altered, and tamed constitute the *vocabulary* of virtuous, classical schooling patterns. All good schooling patterns take advantage of the horse's natural tendencies to avoid work by going *inverted, rapidly* and *sideways*.

The genius of correct classical training strategy is based on the principle of utilizing the horse's natural tendencies, even those that are undesirable, for our purposes. We recognize the horse's escape mechanisms, and harness them by mastering inversion and instead, culturing a horse that is longitudinally flexed and submitting his haunches for the rider's control. We do this by conquering speed through slowing the rhythm, improving the balance and thereby making collection a possibility. We do this by slowing the tempo, rebalancing the horse toward his haunches into collection. We address crookedness by straightening him and insisting on the even use of his hind legs, we help align his torso and redirect the energy of his limbs. Straight, collected, and supple, the athletically effortless carrier of the rider emerges.

Chapter 5
Training Principles

The art of riding is complex. The principles we pursue on a daily basis are the same as those employed for the long-term goal of developing an athletic horse. The principles and the order in which we pursue them are based on an understanding of the training goals.

The goal of all riding should be the development of the horse's athletic talent beyond what he would voluntarily do, and in such a way as to accommodate his carrying the added weight of his rider. In order to carry his rider, the horse must be maintained in nearly perfect balance in motion. In order to develop his athletic potential, we must develop his strength and skills knowledgeably with these goals in mind:

1. The horse's haunches should always be supple and responsive to the rider's aids.
2. The horse should progress with pure and amplified gaits.
3. The horse's center of gravity should be collected toward his haunches, thereby lightening his forehand and stabilizing his carriage. Even during the extension of gaits, the horse should remain collected and anchored in his hocks.
4. The horse should lower his haunches, sink with his croup toward the ground, by tucking his pelvis forward and under, and sinking on strong, elastic joints when impacting on the ground.

These goals must be understood and cultivated during every training session in order to develop the horse consistently, increase his strength and diversify his skills. The means to reach these goals are based on the understanding and correct pursuit of nine major principles, which benefit the horse. The principles should be established in the sequence listed below, yet each of them must be blended, interrelated, and emphasized according to daily varying gymnastic needs.

FIG 5.0 A   **FIG 5.0 B**

FIGURE 5.0 A & B *Observe the difference the rider can achieve by slacking the reins on image 5.0 A. More lowering of haunches with rising forehand. On image 5.0 B one observes more reach and height of the legs usage but a little higher croup. Everything the rider does has meaning to the horse. We should always aid with precision and purpose.*

FIGURE 5.0 C *Here the rider slacks the reins similar to image 5.0 A and achieves the same. lowering of haunches with rising forehand in the medium trot thus proving the benefits of self-cariage in the most ground-gaining trot (5.0C), and the most collected of trots [piaffe] (5.0A) on the same horse.*

FIG 5.0 C

To conquer inversion
1. Relaxation
2. Focus
3. Longitudinal flexion

To conquer speed or sluggish movement
4. Balance
5. Rhythm
6. Impulsion
7. Collection

To conquer crookedness
8. Suppleness
9. Engagement

These training principles developed in order to successfully respond to, and eventually conquer, the horse's three basic escape mechanisms. By inverted body posture, by speeding and by crookedness, the horse can and will avoid the proper mobilization of his musculature and the increased articulation of his joints for the optimum propulsion of his rider.

These principles interact with and relate to the concepts of rehabilitation, therapy, and the athletic development of the horse.

Rehabilitative work includes principles 1 through 5 below, and results in (a) reestablishing the horse's natural balance under the rider's weight, and (b) confirming the purity of the horse's gaits.

Therapeutic work includes principles 6 and 7 above, and results in (a) straightening the horse's torso and aligning his spine, and (b) loading the horse's hind legs evenly and in the direction of his corresponding forehand, and (c) ambidexterity, which is necessary for suppleness and engagement.

Athletic development includes principles 8 and 9 above, and results in amplified gaits and athletic powers expanded to their full potential.

The training principles could be superimposed and must be simultaneously pursued, however, with sequential emphasis. A logical sequential listing is important in order to understand that only one facet of each principle can be emphasized, with the others in supportive roles, during its period of emphasis.

The nine training principles for the achievement of the horse's athletic development require daily repetition. Reinforcement of these concepts gives the schooling of horses a much needed consistency and will ensure the gradual sophistication of each training goal.

The training principles are sequenced as follows and later are addressed more fully in the next chapters.

1. **RELAXATION** is, first of all, a mental state, which in horses is exhibited physically by neuromuscular relaxation. Without this state of mind, no schooling can proceed.

2. **FOCUS** of the horse on the rider must replace his scanning his environment for objects of interest. The horse's mental concentration, when diverted from external environment to internal attention to the rider, allows the rider's aids to meaningfully communicate with the horse. Through mental attention and focus on the rider, the horse will eventually surrender the energy of his haunches to the rider's control.

3. **LONGITUDINAL FLEXION** is essential to avoid injury and pain to the horse and to connect the hocks with the bridle so that the rider controls his horse by the authority of his seat rather than the unnecessary force of the reins. Only through consistent longitudinal flexion, can horses stretch their spine and use the proper set of sympathetic muscles for locomotion, rather than the wrong ones designed for fighting. Only through stretching and flexing the top-line can horses' muscles work in tone without tension. Flexion has three distinct components:

    (a) The *front bascule* consists of the horse's neck arched like a bow over the "bow string" of the rein, allowing his head to hang supplely and perpendicularly from his poll. The top neck muscles flexed parallel the crest of the neck, and as it strengthens, becomes thicker and wider as a result of the horse's progressively sophisticated energy support from his haunches.

    (b) The *middle bascule* is formed by the horse's elevated, rounded back, which swings and articulates loosely, because by flexing his abdominal grid he carries his rider properly. Such an elevated and loose back will transmit the energy emitted by the haunches unhindered to the forehand.

    (c) The hind *bascule* is the most important because it includes the haunches. From the haunches, all energy is issued, and it is there that most of the horse and rider's composite weight should be anchored. The lumbar back should tilt the pelvis forward and under, lowering the point of the croup. The lumbosacral joint is the most difficult to supple because it requires the most time-consuming developmental skills of the horse, engendered by the rider, to cause it to flex. As a result of rounding, flexing, and toning the haunches, horses can compress their bodies, lower their haunches toward the ground, and increase articulation of their joints even when the limbs impact on the ground—not only when they are airborne. Therefore, the limbs can sink softly toward the ground and allow liquid softness to penetrate their structure (figs. 5.1 a–f).

4. **BALANCE** must be maintained at all times and during all developmental stages of a horse. Balance must be monitored by insisting on the same rhythm even while alternating the lengthening and shortening of the horse's strides.

5. **RHYTHM** must be maintained by regulating the horse's footfalls in each gait to an even beat when impacting on the ground. This regularity of rhythm and regularity of footfall must be maintained whether the horse is asked to travel "ruler straight," or bent.

6. **IMPULSION** is the result of the increased activity of the horse's joints by increasing articulation. Strength and suppleness are the result of impulsion, and these qualities allow the horse to move economically, that is, with great activity yet slowly. Impulsion is tamed energy, distributed according to the rider's will. Speed, an escape mechanism, is the *enemy of impulsion*.

7. **COLLECTION** is the shifting of the horse's center of gravity toward his haunches. It liberates the weaker forehand from stress and allows for effortless carriage by increasing suspension, life, and cadence.

8. **SUPPLENESS** refers to the elasticity of muscle use and increased articulation of all the horse's joints. It is proven by an unblocked flow of energy through a toned body without tension. It is also documented by the horse's posture and stride changing and adjusting from the rider's control.

9. **ENGAGEMENT** is a complex concept that includes three objectives:

    (a) Doing better than before.

    (b) Performing the definitive feature of any exercise to the maximum.

    (c) Maintaining performance by the horse until changed by the rider.

The Vocabulary of Athletic Development

This is an enormously important and visually educating photo essay. It conveys one of the most important principles of riding, which is that the fulfillment of the athletic goals required from the horse is based on his posture and gaits being adjustable. These should be delicately adjusted with an infinite number of continuous possibilities. The horse's limb movements, body stretching or contracting, posture, and lateral oscillation, should all be at the rider's disposal for stride-by-stride adjustment.

A horse on the aids is not just minimally controllable. The sophistication of training and suppleness depend on, and are evaluated by, the rider's ability to display the horse's adjustability. The perpetual changeability of the horse's stride and posture is the very definition and demonstrable documentation of his suppleness. There are no movements to perform, only exercises to be done.

The sequence of these pictures is all the more fabulous because it communicates a continuum of trotting action being photographed at the beginning of changes from one kind of trot to another. Observe the lowering of the haunches and the rising at

FIG 5.1 A　　　　　　　　　　　　　　**FIG 5.1 B**

FIGURE 5.1 A *This photo shows the maximum seating of the horse—lowering the haunches and raising the withers—to begin the piaffe, a trot so masterfully engaged as to increase activity of the haunches without progressing in space.*

FIGURE 5.1 B *This picture shows the commencement of the passage. This trot is made majestic with each stride having maximum lift with minimal progression, demonstrating that increased impulsion results in decreased speed. Cadence, elevation of stride, loftiness of carriage, and eloquent "body bouncing" prove that when increased activity of the haunches is infused with great impulsion, a gravity-defying floating of the horse's majestic body is obtainable.*

FIG 5.1 C　　　　　　　　　　　　　　**FIG 5.1 D**

FIGURE 5.1 C *Here, the passage is being energized for the next photo* **5.1 D**, *which is the first step of the medium trot. Note that a well-developed horse can demonstrate the principle that the passage is the most collected medium trot, and that a perfect medium trot is a hugely stretched passage. By this, I mean that in the medium trot, the horse elastically extends his stride without losing his majestic suspension, resulting in a slow-motion, highly elevated, grandly articulated, and greatly stretched passage-like action.*

FIG 5.1 E   FIG 5.1 F

FIGURE 5.1 E *The medium trot is transitioning toward the extended trot, and is showing the great power reserves that allow the lowering of the haunches to "take off up hill" in full extension as shown in 5.1 F.*

The principle of a seamless continuum from the most collected to the most extended trot is supported by the observation that the haunches are always "closed," meaning lowered, and that the point of the croup is always sinking toward the ground.

The horse is always moving "uphill," with his withers higher than his croup, and the poll higher than his withers. Furthermore, his weight remains obviously in the haunches. Therefore, the horse is collected. This demonstrates that the medium and extended gaits—while longer in stride and greater in stretching of the limbs—do not include any change of the center of gravity toward the forehand, nor is there any resultant rushing.

All exercises must remain anchored in the haunches. The joints of the hindquarters should show flexion, not only when airborne, but also while impacting on the ground. In these photos, you can see the flexibility and strength of the joints, and that all the transitions are "powered" by very flexible haunches.

Notice that the contact is something the horse does, not the rider. The rider maintains her horse in balance, using her seat and never her hands. Her shoulders, upper arms, and elbows define her seat. Imagine a balancing scale: the rider is the center, and the two scales on either side of her are rising and falling with the scale always heavier on the haunches' side, and lighter on the forehand's.

the withers. Regardless of the length of stride, the horse remains collected and seated. Elizabeth Ball is riding.

The correct posture and deportment of the horse is indispensable to his athletic development. In every stage of training, the posture must be slightly different because it is a result of proper transmission of energy from the haunches. In any day of work and in executing different exercises, the horse will use his haunches differently and transmit his energy in various ways, primarily dependent on correct riding (fig. 5.2).

Care must be taken that when energizing the horse's haunches, the first energy the rider receives, must be used to create correct *posture*. That posture, of course, is always in proper longitudinal flexion but varies as to the length and height of the horse's carriage; this determines the location of the horse's center of gravity. The center of gravity can shift up or down, of course, as well as toward the forehand or the haunches. The correct posture at the halt should be transferable when the horse is in motion. Energy procured from the haunches beyond the establishment of *posture* and creation of deportment may now be spent on *transportation*.

The deportment of the horse signals his readiness to submit his haunches to work. Only when the postural muscles are flexed can the horse be "on the aids" because this principle is based on the horse's willingness to surrender to the rider's control. When a horse is "on the aids," the rider can control not only the *direction* of his progress, but also his *location* in space. In addition, the rider can control *how* the horse is progressing through space: his rhythm, tempo, straightness, degree of collection, and level of engagement.

When the horse moves in correct posture, commensurate with the engagement of his haunches, we can observe, and see in photographs as well, that the horse's front and hind legs appear to form a triangle and the triangles are equal in size and shape. Should the front triangle be larger or different in shape than the one formed by the hind legs, the horse is said to be disunited, out of balance, and in the wrong posture usually because of being confined through his neck.

Lateral bending cannot take place without longitudinal flexion.

The rider ought to understand the difference between postural and locomotive muscles. Postural muscles give stability to the horse's carriage, and allow the rider to balance and control the horse's entire body. Locomotive muscles offer transportation by controlling the movements of the limbs, and can function correctly only after the postural muscles have been flexed correctly.

Locomotion in a false flexion is the result of disengagement of the postural muscle elements:

(a) The nuchal ligament, which runs along the top-line.

(b) The psoas muscles, which contribute to raising the knees and the hocks.

(c) The neck and abdominal muscles flexed show a "trough" line as proof of delineation of the muscles flexing and contracting.

The horse that is allowed, or worse yet, encouraged to rush, will escape by fulfilling those functions that are properly the domain of the postural muscles with the muscles of locomotion, which push and pull instead. If this be allowed to happen, the horse will ruin his locomotion and change the cellular structure of his muscles. Great harm, and lack of suppleness will certainly follow.

Escape Mechanism*	Remedy**	Task	Goal
Inversion	Relaxation Focus Longitudinal Flexon	**REHABILITATION** Establish: Natural Balance Purity of Gaits	**AMPLIFICATION OF GAITS** Ground-Gaining Stride Suspension Freedom and Looseness Agility
Speed	Balance Rhythm Impulsion Collection	**THERAPEUTIC WORK** Establish: Straightening Even Loading Ambidexterity	
Crookedness	Suppleness Engagement	**ATHLETIC DEVELOPMENT** Establish: Changeability and adjustability to control where, when, and how	

* The horse's natural, inborn evasions to working with his haunches.

** The process of training is simply to conquer the evasions in order to develop potential by giving the horse sufficient strength and skills.

FIG 5.2

Chapter 6
Rehabilitative Work

The five training principles I discuss in this chapter are particularly effective in rehabilitative work. Relaxation is fundamental to any physical activity.

Relaxation

Relaxation will always include, even at a minimal level, the absence of tension. Mental tranquility will manifest itself in physical (neuromuscular) relaxation, and if minimal relaxation is consistently maintained by the rider, it will gradually and eventually allow the horse the sophistication necessary for moving with tone. Thus, omission of tension results in the commission of tone.

With any horse, most of the rider's attention should be directed to the creation and maintenance of tranquility. Later, through a gradual progression toward the most sophisticated level, this will manifest itself in engagement. The conceptual circle from the relaxation of a horse to the tone of an engaged horse is closed by work on all the integral concepts of *balance, rhythm,* and *impulsion.*

Relaxation is the alpha and omega of all sophisticated riding.

Relaxation also implies the absence of fear, which means the horse trusts his rider and is attentive to him. When the horse's occasional attention to the rider's strong aids evolves into his undivided attention to the slightest aids, and he focuses absolutely on his rider, the horse will have supplanted his instinct-guided, inherited behavior with one that is at the disposal of the rider.

Physical relaxation is manifested by the horse becoming a cohesive athletic system, capable of carrying his rider with ease unharmed by the effort, and at the same time accessible and controllable.

This behavioral focus on, and surrender to, the rider's will is evidenced physically in the posture of longitudinal flexion. As always, mental readiness makes physical manifestation possible. Observation of the structure and physiology of the horse leads us to the realization that nature made him a creature unable to carry any weight on top of himself without stress, pain, and discomfort causing a gradual, yet constant process of physical breakdown. This regrettable scenario, however, can, and must be prevented by allowing, inviting, and guiding each horse to acquire the posture of longitudinal flexion.

Only by carrying his rider in a flexed posture can the horse find his work pain less, and with progress through the phases of balance, rhythm, impulsion and engagement, even pleasurable.

FIGURE 6.0 *The moment of a "strike off" into left lead canter. The outside hind leg supports the entire combined weight of horse and rider. The horse is in collection with the outside hind leg supporting in a vertical pillar-like position. The inside hind leg is poised to support deeply under with the left hock poised to reach level with the outside stifle. The horse's pelvis is tilted forward with the croup compressing toward the ground as the strong and supple joints in the haunches articulate fully. The forehand is clearly unburdened with the withers rising. The head and neck are positioned in correct poise. Jessica Jo Tate riding.*

Focus and Contact

Contact refers to a great deal more than the usual perception that it is merely the rider's hands holding a pair of reins attached to a bit. This suggests that contact is always and only with the horse's mouth. A grave mistake. Contact refers to the entire proposition of a partnership between horse and rider. It also has two distinct aspects, that of a physical and a mental contact with our horses. Physical contact includes all surfaces where the two creatures, horse and rider, touch or sense each other. These, of course, include the rider's seat, legs, and hands extending through reins to affect the bit.

Mental contact is based on the rider's expectation that the horse will first pay attention, later focus more consistently, and finally, submit totally to his will and guidance. Clearly, the rider must earn the horse's confidence by behaving justly, lovingly, and respectfully toward him and by communicating to him through the aids with consistency and clarity.

All rules concerning correct contact can be suspended during an emergency. A startled, frightened, disobedient horse that has reverted to his instinctive reactions can cause great harm to his rider and even himself, however unwittingly, and without conspiratorial wickedness. A horse in nature must rely on his genetically coded instinctive responses for his survival. When he is instinctively pursuing his survival, he cannot pay attention to his rider's safety, comfort, and composure.

However, our discussion must be limited to the good times when horses pay attention to their riders and through development of the attention span come to focus consistently on a rider's contact and communication efforts.

When a rider assumes contact with his horse, he should start it with his legs, which command the horse's energy, which matures to impulsion. The rider's legs energize the horse, his seat modifies the energizing effects, and the reins verify to the horse that his performance is approved. There is much to remember about the rationality of this order of contacting. To repeat this in a slogan that is easy to remember:

Legs energize, seat modifies, reins verify.

The legs energize the horse to create impulsion, they bend the horse to supple him, and aid in the rhythm desired to sustain the horse's energy and engagement. The authority of the rider's adhesive seat moving with the horse's gaits stabilizes the balance created by the propulsive energy. The seat contributes to the rhythmic regularity by its vertical and lateral activities that join the horse's motion as if dancing in partnership with him. The seat also determines the gait for which the legs are to be energized. All energy modification is seat based. The hands merely transmit the rider's seat effects to the horse's mouth—the termination point of the horse's longitudinal flexion. The energy of the haunches arrives in the bridle in a transmuted form that conveys to the horse the rider's mind, verifying displeasure or approval of his progression. Educated hands are quiet because they are independent of the horse's jolting and jarring caused by his impact on the ground. The rider's hands must remain motionless relative to the horse's perpetual motion and oscillation, rather than motionless relative to the ground on which the horse travels. In order to be quiet, educated hands make movements by the will and the design of the rider for the purposeful transmission of the seat's messages to the bridle. The hands must remain the extension of the seat by which the horse can "read the rider's mind."

In order to effect the reins' contact correctly, riders ought to remember three principles:

First, the contact is made by the horse and not by the rider. Therefore, the rider should merely present a motionless bit. This is achieved by a passive resistance to any movement in the rider's upper arm, elbow, and fist for a brief period of time, determined by the horse's reaction. Once the horse senses the perimeter of his flexion as defined by the passive presentation of the bit, which establishes the bit's relationship to the perpendicular downward pressure of the rider's seat, he can step up to the bit by connecting the energy of his hocks, through stretching and lifting his back, into the bridle. As soon as the flexion occurs, the horse's neck arches. The rider must immediately verify and confirm the correctness and desirability of the flexion to the

FIG 6.1 A **FIG 6.1 B**

FIGURES 6.1 A & B *Arthur Kottas-Heldenberg, First Chief Rider of the Spanish Riding School in Vienna, Austria, and his daughter, Caroline Kottas-Heldenberg who is a successful competitor and trainer, are riding the extended trot, the crowning achievement of longitudinal flexion.*

In 6.1 A The younger horse is extending the trot in a horizontal balance. In 6.1 B, this horse, more gymnastically advanced, is extending the trot "more uphill." Notice, however, that both horses work with the top neck muscles flexed through, well-defined, and visible all the way to their shoulders. Their legs are synchronized and form even triangles. The joints in the limbs are well flexed. The shoulders are free to fully extend their reach. The tails are hanging, and there is no sign of tension. Even the horses' ears, eyes, and faces express full attention to, and confidence in the riders. The riders' aids are invisible, and are obviously not hindering, confining, or interfering with their horses.

horse, by yielding forward on the reins just enough to accommodate the movements of the muscle groups affected, especially in the forearms and neck.

Second, the horse will contact the bit. The rider's job ends with a deep seat and arms steady to present the bit. Thereafter, the rider may feel only the combined weight of the bit and the reins. If the horse were to pull, the rider should offer passive resistance rather than active pulling, sawing, or jerking on the mouth. Passive resistance will increase the rider's seat authority as downward pressure on the horse's spine increases. Passive resistance instructs the horse that pulling on the reins, instead of dislodging the rider's seat, amplifies it and compels him to step under the rider's center of gravity with greater energy from the hocks. By engaging his haunches, the horse necessarily lightens the contact and chews on the bit, relaxing his muscles, especially in the neck.

Third, is the principle that the rider may hold only the weight of the reins and the bit hanging on its end. This means that the rider should not pull on the reins, and therefore, not pull on the horse. Pulling provokes the horse's instinctive claustrophobia and makes him pull even more in an attempt to extricate himself from confinement. The reins should also not hinder the ground-gaining flow of limb movements, nor should it inhibit impulsion, but rather keep the doors open to flawless, seamless, liquid, light, suspended, liberated, forward progression.

No horse understands the meaning of rein contact instinctively. This is learned over time. The way it is taught is the way it will be learned. The rider who complains about his horse pulling on his arms is riding a horse that is complaining of a rider pulling his mouth. It takes two to pull. No one can pull on a rope whose end is not tied to something. No amount of pulling will slow or balance a horse, because the pulling rider continues to travel on the legs of the pulled horse. So he goes where those horse legs take him and at the rate of speed that the frightened and hurt horse decides to take him. Naturally, horses run from pain. Consequently, pain caused by pulling on the rein can cause a horse to run away with the rider.

Contact is much more than the skill of handling the reins properly. It is the total reciprocal involvement between horse and rider. Contact is as much created by the horse as it is invited by the rider. It results in a dialogue, in reciprocal and reciprocated signals, and in two-way communication. It results in the harmony that issues from the stability of two living things in constant communication with one another.

The terms accepted by the equestrian culture about "rein contact" and "the horse on the bit" are among the most misunderstood and should be discussed in some detail.

The Horse on the Bit—an Explanation:

The "horse on the bit" is an unfortunate expression because it is potentially misleading. Long accepted as part of the classical idiom, its use will most certainly continue. There may have been times when consensus was possible because those who used terms or expressions understood their colloquial meaning. Now that equestrian educational backgrounds are increasingly diverse and the number of riders is considerably greater, equestrian understanding of terminology differs depending on the source from which it was acquired.

If one were to test the phrase "horse on the bit" on people not involved in riding, they might interpret its meaning in unfortunate ways. Their concept might not be too far from picturing a parrot on a stick. And they would, sadly, be quite right in view of how many riders really aim to force their horses to perch on the bit much like a bird on a perch. Therefore, it is worth offering some thoughts on this important phrase and the subject it suggests.

A definition of the concept includes a horse that is longitudinally flexed by stretching his top-line and expanding his spinal column allowing the energy of his hindquarters to travel unencumbered through his entirety without blocking the flow by tension in his muscles (figs. 6.1 a & b). A longitudinally stretched horse is flexed as a by-product of being stretched. However, flexion is not sufficient to produce the correct equine movement unless it is integral to stretching the spine. This is done by means of stretching the nuchal cord—a ligament that spans the horse's length from poll to the dock of the tail.

A result of spinal stretching is the horse's ability to flex the system of muscles indispensable to correct locomotion and carriage under the rider's weight. These muscles work together in a complex system of *sympathetic responses*—when one of these muscles is flexed, a group of others join it and also flex. The horse's top neck muscle is one of several muscles participating in the sympathetic response system. If the rider succeeds in flexing that muscle instead of only flexing the horse at the poll (which is a joint with no ability to expand or contract as muscles do) the rest of its sympathetic muscle group will also flex (fig. 6.2). These include the abdominal muscles that carry

FIGURE 6.2 *The author is yielding the rein to show that a horse can flex the neck correctly without rein pressure.*

the rider's weight and allow continued freedom of articulation of the back muscles (swinging as energy transmits through them unhindered) and the muscles in the croup and buttocks that push the stifle joint forward and upward.

The rider can activate the flexion and elasticity of this important sympathetic muscle group by either starting with the relaxation of the horse's neck, sending his neck and head forward and downward, or by sustaining his posture but increasing the activity in the muscles of the haunches, which propel the stifles and convey the energy of the hocks.

The rider can create the flexing of the horse's top muscles that induces longitudinal flexion and relaxation through stretching, by starting either at the horse's front (most suitable for tense and fast horses) or at his haunches (most suitable for lazy, sluggish, weak and slow horses). In either case, the rider needs to also stretch the horse, not merely to flex him. Flexion without stretch is possible by a short, tense, inhibited horse but not advisable. Stretching eradicates tension and alleviates inhibitions to movement and posture.

FIGURE 6.3 A *Frances Williams demonstrates the full yield of both reins in the medium trot on the diagonal to verify and test Centauro for self-carriage, straightness and balance.*

FIGURE 6.3 B *The author is correctly stretching the horse "long and low." This stretching of the horse forward and down is done by lengthening the reins, long enough for the horse "to fill it up with energy from the hind-legs."*

Flexing the poll is not a goal. By itself, flexing the poll is useless. However, when the proper muscles are flexed through their stretching, the poll will also necessarily flex as a by-product of complete longitudinal flexion. Flexion at the poll does not induce longitudinal stretching and flexion at the poll is valid only as an by-product of longitudinal stretching (figs. 6.3 a & b).

Correct longitudinal stretching rounds the top-line and enables the horse to move in his entirety, not just with the legs. The same stretching enables the horse to absorb the shock that is caused by his impact on the ground.

None of the above is possible if the horse is "nailed to the bit." By nature, the horse is a claustrophobic creature that will "break out of bondage" at any cost. Instinctively, he will respond to pressure with counter pressure. The rider that pulls on his mouth will be countered by a horse that pulls on the bit. Confining and restricting hands will cause the horse to activate his entire body to pull against the rider. Muscles tense, ligaments stress and joints stiffen, the horse will use all his strength and power to fight confinement. When subjected to painful intrusion rather than the pleasurable activities of eating and drinking, the horse's mouth can produce enormous tension in the entire body of horse. Tension will not be limited to the physical effort to "break out of bondage" but will appear in anxiety-induced behavior: shying, bolting, kicking, grinding the teeth, pulling the lips up, clattering teeth, sucking the tongue back, hanging the tongue out of the mouth, and all unsightly and auditory signals of distress.

Horses "nailed to the bit" will naturally respond by first stiffening their muscles, then their joints. This will result in deterioration, not enhancement of the basic gaits. We will see unsuspended, choppy, shuffling strides, the very antithesis of amplified, suspended, elastic movements of softness and easy grandeur.

In Review

Let us review what is really meant by the phrase that refers to ***the horse on the bit***.

- The contact is something the horse does, not the rider!
- The rider merely teaches, encourages, and tutors the horse to contact the bit.
- The horse's efforts should be encouraged by yielding with the hands forward, providing for an expansion of the frame and the lengthening of the neck.
- After the horse contacts the bit, the hands should become passive, stable yet soft, to confirm and reward the horse's action.
- The expression "the horse on the bit" comes from the age-old understanding that the horse contacts the bit, not the rider's hands, arms and, heaven forbid, his entire torso by leaning and pulling on it.
- The horse contacts the bit, which must hang, and not be pulled against the jaw, in his mouth. The horse contacts the bit with his hocks, not with his mouth, with which he merely eats and drinks under natural circumstances.

- The horse should seek a contact with the bit precisely because the rider liberates rather than confines him through his contact.
- By yielding on the reins, the rider lets the horse know that his correct contact will not confine his frame and inhibit his strides.

He who misunderstands this concept, however, will pull on the horse's mouth, and cause the horse to strain against his entire body, arms, and hands. Such a tormented horse will be compelled to extricate himself from his unnatural confinement. This perpetuated physical stress puts the horse on a muscle system unsuitable for the improvement of his locomotion. Instead of his posture being a result of the engagement of his quarters, his forced and confined posture inhibits the use of his haunches.

The entire point of gymnastic development is negated by pulling hands.

A pulling rider becomes the nemesis, not the mentor of the horse. This type of rider renounces the aids, and chooses destruction of his horse.

The purpose of allowing the horse to seek and contact the bit is to form a termination point that defines the limit of the horse's stretching and invites him to feel the termination point of his energy. This enables the rider to communicate his wishes through his seat to the horse's forehand. Through the authority of his seat, the rider can succeed in creating the horse's desired posture, carriage, speed, and cadence because his energy is harnessed from the haunches. By contacting the bit, the horse should become aware of his rider's mind, better understand his intentions, and even sense through this contact with the bit the activities of the rider's seat.

In order for the seat to communicate to the bit, the rider must sit in the correct posture. This must include a perpendicularly positioned upper arm and a still elbow, all of which hanging from a flat position of the shoulder blades. This posture can be described as a straight, erect torso with a stretched spine, shoulder folded back and down, with the rib cage lifted out of the abdominal cavity. This posture and arm position helps to sustain a passive, isometric resistance to involuntary movements by the hands, and instability in the isometric tone of the torso. This will enable the horse to "step through" the rider's torso and monitor his adhesive seat. The rider's seat is comprised of many more elements than his seat bones and buttocks. The combined effects of the seat, when driving or in passive resistance are far more effective than the separate elements of the seat used in isolation.

The effect of seat is much more than the sum of its parts (gestalt[2]) because it includes the manner in which these parts interrelate from moment to moment.

Contact is *definitely not*:
- A feeling of force connecting a human fist with an equine jaw.
- A sense of holding a wall against which to push the horse.
- A point of inhibition to the liberty of movement in the haunches and forehand.

---

[2] gestalt: an organized whole that is perceived as more than the sum of its parts. Oxford Dictionary. - Editor's note.

- A point of confinement that can force the horse to invert his neck and by doing that, infuse tension to all other sympathetic muscles.
- A point of pressure or a sense of anchoring a horse, around which he can desperately pivot by "fishtailing" with his haunches.
- A fifth leg on which he can lean as if on a crutch.

The recommendation for the tender maintenance of steady rein contact comes from riding fast across open country and by jumping. Such steady reins prevent abrupt and punitive use. They should feel like silk cords that should not be torn.

Longitudinal Flexion

Longitudinal flexion is the key concept to classical horsemanship because it provides us with a pain-free horse, and one integrated into an energy system controllable from both ends by the rider at its center. The flexed horse becomes a bridge, full of a soft, swinging transmission of energy through its entire span from its anchor at the hocks to the bridle.

The concept of longitudinal flexion is at the heart of classical horsemanship. Its production, maintenance, and control are the prerequisites to all training and guarantee schooling progress. Classical equitation belongs to a special equine galaxy, light years away from all other riding fashions and whims because of its understanding of, insisting on, and employing longitudinal flexion.

Longitudinal flexion makes it possible for the horse to transport his rider painlessly and without physical stress to himself. Otherwise, the horse's impact on (contact with) the ground as he moves with the rider's added weight on his back would cause him pain and injury. Having flexed, the horse arranges a posture with specific muscular contractions and stretching that insures that the contact with the ground is distributed throughout his body without jarring him. The movement is evenly distributed throughout the horse's body and no point of tension or trauma develops.

The horse must come into a flexed posture by stretching his entire spine from tail to poll to the greatest extent possible, thereby making the spine itself supple and causing no stress to the vertebrae. Flexion without spinal stretch is useless and false. Muscles place the skeleton. The horse's muscles must be able to stretch and contract to enable movement with a stretched and flexible (longitudinally swinging and laterally bending) spine.

Through longitudinal flexion, the rider gains control of the horse's haunches. By passive resistance, the rider suggests to the horse that he slow the spatial progress of his forehand relative to the progression of his haunches. This allows the horse to bring his hind legs closer to his muzzle, step more under his center of gravity, shorten his posture, and move as a closed, comprehensive energy system from hocks to the bit.

Only a longitudinally flexed horse can tuck his pelvis under and flex his joints efficiently. This not only saves him from injury, but also gives the rider the chance to improve the horse's gaits by amplifying them. For schooling purposes, horses must learn to stretch and contract their bodies in a continuous manner, and, as a separate function, to lengthen and shorten their strides on a continuum. A correctly trained horse makes these two adjustments available to the rider, enabling him to "adjust his dials" to find the combination of stride length and body posture that are ideal for the performance of any particular school movement. Only a supple horse can progress in the perfection of his gaits in the collected, medium, and extended modes.

All classical schooling is progressive. Each concept is schooled through an evolutionary process often from meager beginnings, through gradual development, to maximum efficiency. Therefore, the horse's longitudinal flexion is also time dependent and its sophistication is a concern synonymous with classical equitation.

Balance and Its Evolution to Collection

The horse that lost his balance is not with us. As I mentioned before, historically, an unbalanced horse was eaten by a predator. "The survival of the fittest" gave us horses with the genes to guard against imbalance.

The rider's presence on the horse's back directly threatens the horse's genetically coded sense of safety because the alien weight upsets the horse's balance. The rider creates imbalance and triggers an instinctive reminder of danger to the horse. The rider is a death warning to the horse. This burdens the rider (often unwittingly) with a heavy debt. We owe the horse our assistance in rebalancing.

Recall that longitudinal flexion through stretching is indispensable to all ridden horses for the prevention of neuromuscular injury, ligamental stress, and skeletal trauma. Remember that longitudinal flexion is the rider's only way to apologize for sitting on a horse that was not made for carrying a burden on his back.

It is the duty of the rider to apologize for our life-threatening appearance on the horse's back that upsets his natural balance. After the urgent need for longitudinal flexion, we must proceed with the task of improving the horse's balance under our weight. This task is gradual and the balancing ability of the horse should increase with his schooling and straightening.

Finally, the horse's balance ought to become more sophisticated and surpass what the horse would voluntarily produce in nature, without human assistance. Only a rider who has acquired a balanced seat can hope to improve the horse's balance. Riders not yet correctly balanced cannot improve any horse's schooling because they will disturb horses' flexion with involuntary hand actions and disturb the horse's balance by falling away from the horse's center of gravity (figs. 6.4 a & b).

Balancing a horse is based on the prerequisite longitudinal flexion, and is also a new dimension for its sophistication. It is through the balancing properties of the half-halt and the full halt that we begin to address the horse's "hind bascule." The ultimate goal of schooling horses includes the achievement of collection, which means the haunches assume more of the composite weight of horse and rider. Collection depends on and manifests itself in the horse's skill and strength in using his abdominal muscles to round his lumbar back behind the saddle. Consequently, he tilts his pelvis forward, lowers his croup by flexing the lumbosacral joint, and anchors himself at the pelvis for the carriage of his rider. This postural change, by increased strength and flexion behind the saddle, is the "hind bascule," and it is dependent upon the horse's using his joints in increased articulation. A collected horse, seated over a forward-tilted pelvis,

FIGURES 6.4 A & B *The proof of sophisticated balance is to raise the horse's back and deepen the flexion in every movement. In 6.4 A, the horse is in medium trot, and in 6.4 B, he is in collected trot. The rider is deepening the position of his horse's poll, and is raising the horse's back. This activity need not last longer than two strides, but may be pursued longer if necessary. Elasticity, suppleness, and "through-ness" are dependent on, and confirmed by changeability of the horse's posture. This includes the adjustability of the top-line, the posture, the length of stride, and the degree of bending. The deepening of the poll is a stretching exercise, and en- tirely dependent on yielding reins and driving.*

will softly rotate and flex his joints, not only when his limbs are airborne, but also when they impact on the ground, assuming full weight-bearing responsibilities. Thus, a collected, supple, and well-seated horse will impact on the ground with the softness of a snowflake. He will no longer "drive nails into the soil," because his hooves will be able to alight softly by sinking on his straightened, supple joints.

I hope riders will understand that while flexion begins with the instruction of the horse to stretch and lengthen his body, it must be done with roundness. It is the "front bascule" that is indispensable for the beginning of all flexion through stretch, and it must be frequently reviewed on a daily basis. Yet, the ultimate goal is not to be complacent about controlling the horse's forehand and the navigational equipment of his neck and head. But rather, having securely established the front bascule we can enter the magical world of balancing and rebalancing the horse with a dedication to shifting his center of gravity toward his haunches and with it, taking weight off the sensitive forehand so prone to injuries.

By now, you surely detect that balance is an ever-changing situation and that it varies on a long continuum of sophistication from a horse "falling on his forehand" to one anchored fully over his hind legs and folded under on gathered haunches. The continuum of balancing horses toward their haunches should be varied. For it is in the changing of the flexion of the horse, as well as the changing of his balance to varying degrees toward his haunches, that we produce suppleness. Supple, liquid, unlocked fluency of efficient movement comes through the magic of changes. Horses ridden "nailed into the same frame," and "hurried briskly in (so-called!) impulsion," will never become supple. Instead, they are being drilled in the efficiencies of rigid posturing and avoidance of work with the haunches by evasion. Horses that do not want to work will flee off their haunches to their forehand by two evasions: speed and crookedness.

FIG 6.5 A   FIG 6.5 B

FIGURE 6.5 A *Aesthetic and artistic appeal depend on correct gymnastic content. Notice the trot, when engaged and cadenced, has high limb action, and the front hoof is lifted twice as high as the hind hoof. From the haunches, the horse rises toward the withers. The upper neck muscle is well flexed and parallel with the top-line on the crest. The lower neck muscle under the flexing top neck muscle shows that it is being used correctly from the top of the throat latch all the way to the shoulder blade. Sonja Vracko is riding.*

FIGURE 6.5 B *Notice the completely correct uphill canter. The horse is anchored on the starting leg of the canter. This outside hind leg is impacting on the ground and is the sole support for the entire horse and rider's combined weight at this moment. This leg is strong, supple, and sinking. The hips are lowered, the pelvis tilted forward as the inside hind leg articulates with deep inward motion to support the center of gravity. The horse's whole torso is lifted up by the back and abdominal muscles. This facilitates the raising of the withers and liberates the shoulders. The outside forehand is remark- ably correct—very free and straight with the hoof floating way above the ground. The inside lead leg is very well bent. The shoulder is free, and the cannon bone lifted vertically. These two photos communicate the concept of a horse engaged behind—to sit and anchor—consequently, the forehand is lifted, the shoulders are liberated, and the horse works on an uphill trajectory. Lifting not pushing to carry. Sonja Vracko is the rider.*

Therefore, riders ought to understand that a horse stretched to the maximum, moving with his nose forward and down, near the ground, is not necessarily on the forehand, while horses with their poll raised to the level of the rider's eyebrows may well be! For being on the forehand, of course, is dependent entirely on the degree of the horse's balance and activity with his haunches. In short, head high or low, neck longer or shorter, by themselves, do not speak clearly about the whereabouts of the horse's balance. An educated eye scans not only the neck and head but also the joints in the haunches, the posture, use of the lumbar back, the muscular disposition throughout the top-line, and the velocity and manner of traveling.

Balance is worked on, developed by, and tested with transitions, especially from one gait to another. It is also at the heart of correct bending, even if ever so briefly while traveling through a corner. If a horse cannot move while bending in the same balance as he did before, he speeds, slows or shortens his stride, or denies bending by not stepping with his hind legs toward the direction of his forelegs on the same side, he is in need of rebalancing.

Frequently our attention is diverted to discussions about "artistic riding" as opposed to "competition riding." To repeat, there is only one correct way of riding and if it displays good "content," it is automatically artistically beautiful. Beautiful or artistic riding is perceived as that which produces correct behavior, responses, and performance from the horse. Balance is at the heart of "artistic" riding, and therefore automatically "competition" riding, too. For without balancing a horse under the foreign weight of his rider, the horse is genetically programmed to flee from death and has no time to share with us his abilities for cultured, amplified, grandiloquent gaits (figs. 6.5 a & b).

Rhythm

The horse's rhythm ought to be felt by the rider. Observers and riders alike will see and hear rhythm, which is marked by his footfall. The regularity of the horse's rhythm is essential to his gymnastic development. The recognition that regularity safeguards the horse's athletic development is, like longitudinal flexion and collection, among the distinctive attributes that put classical equitation into a realm of its own, ideologically apart from other ways of riding. For without regularity of footfall, the horse can evade work with his haunches, from which is born the strength and skill that guarantee athletic progress.

All horses are born lopsided, "left-handed" mostly, unlike most human beings, who are born right-handed. Therefore, horses will use their limbs with "unlevel" strides or progress with irregular gaits. The regularity of the horse's footfall must be as reliable as the beat of a drummer. Indeed, the rider's musical talents, his feelings for rhythm are essential for the guarding of the horse's regularity and for the cultivation of his progress through the security of a regular rhythm.

Each horse is born with a "signature rhythm" in his each of his gaits: walk, trot, and canter. Nature largely defined these for him by his physical conformation and mental tendencies toward a phlegmatic or alert disposition. Talented riders and educated coaches easily discern the horse's natural signature rhythm, which is as unique and distinct as human fingerprints. No horse should be driven past, or allowed to linger below the level of his natural rhythm.

Riding talent is comprised of many components, among which the sense of rhythm is one of the most important. We often emphasize that riding talent is dependent on an athletic riding figure, muscle tone, and coordination. Those are lovely and useful attributes, also aesthetically pleasing, yet none is so important as the rider's feeling for rhythm. Only through rhythmic aids can a horse discern the rider's will. Aids applied out of phase with his footfall are not understood. Dullness of sides, souring of the sensory mechanisms and sullen, sad, bitter mental attitudes develop in horses that are badgered by human aids meted out without regard for the rhythm of the footfall. All effective aids become easily discernible because of their rhythmic clarity of delivery. In great riding academies, such as the Spanish Riding School of Vienna, special attention is devoted to the development of the rider's "feel" for which hind leg of the horse is airborne, and which is impacting on the ground to support his weight.

Unless the rider can internalize the feelings for such movement, he cannot deliver aids "on autopilot." Feeling for rhythm comes as naturally to a good rider as do respiration and the blinking of the eyes. All pleasant, inconspicuous, and clear aids are the result of their timely delivery. Aid-efficiency is not strength, but rather rhythm-dependent.

In earlier chapters, I noted that the horse uses two major evasions of work with the haunches. These are dependent on his efficacy in changing the rhythm (slowing or rushing), or to travel crookedly. Straightening of the horse (that is aligning his spinal position parallel to the pattern traveled on the ground) is essential to the maintenance of rhythmic regularity. Therefore, rhythm, flexion, and bending are interdependent. The rider's awareness of rhythmic regularity offers a chance for the straightening of the horse. Without regularity of rhythm, even longitudinal flexion becomes inconsistent and balance disintegrates. Regularity of rhythm is dependent on the preceding conceptual training stages of flexion and balance and, in turn, contributes to their further sophistication. It is against the metronomic regularity of the footfall that riders measure the horse's athletic progress in lengthening and elevating (suspending) his strides. If any driving results in *haste* rather than in increased length or elevation of strides, *progress will be denied* by the horse's evasion. Rhythm must not only remain regular, but also be at the desired rate. This provides the accurate traveling tempo for each horse.

Regularity of footfall can also be too slow or too fast. Riders must insist on a rhythmic regularity that is natural for their horse. That is his "fingerprint." Ultimately, when the rhythmic regularity of the movement is established, it is complemented by the horse's strength and skill to extend and collect his strides. Then, we will have arrived at one of our training goals. The horse will be able to travel in all his gaits in these four distinct designations: working, medium, extended, and collected. All four modes will be amplified over what he would perform naturally. An athletically developed horse will give his rider the great pleasure of rhythmic security. His medium trot will be his longest "passage," and his "passage" will be his collected medium trot. For the same reason, his "piaffe" will be the highest collection of the collected trot as will his collected trot represent merely a ground-gaining "piaffe."

While the rest of the equestrian world travels in fits and starts, jerks and jolts, an experience something like riding in "bumper cars" at an amusement park, riders of classical schooling will glide confidently in the predictable evenness and regularity of a great dancer. Among the riding ecstasies of experiencing periodic weightlessness and the trance of effortlessly gliding through space, we find a rhythm as evenly reliable as a heartbeat, mesmerizing.

Chapter 7
Therapeutic Work

Speed in a horse, while desirable in certain disciplines, is an anathema in dressage—
an evasion mechanism that needs to be addressed.
The rider can do so by working with his horse to increase impulsion—
the source of strength, carrying, and suspension.

Impulsion

Impulsion is the increased activity in the joints of the horse's hindquarters. It is based on careful and gradual development in the articulation (flexion and rotation) of the horse's joints, resulting in supple (therefore strong), and even use of the joints. Impulsion results in a vision of an animated horse progressing slowly, gracefully, and with efficiency of stride. It makes his motion appear majestic.

Impulsion enables the riding horse to do five important things:

1. Through impulsion the horse can progress with minimum effort (energy efficiency) because of an improved balance secured by increased articulation of his joints.
2. The horse can lift and carry (rather than shuffle and push) his rider and himself.
3. He can reduce the jarring effects of his impact on the ground. Because of the increased articulation, born of strength, the joints cannot only lift from, but also sink toward the ground to lessen the impact when striking it.
4. Impulsion protects the horse's anatomy by allowing him to carry his rider softly, minimizing potential physical trauma to both.
5. A horse moving in good impulsion delivers transportation in a measured rhythm.

Speed is the enemy of impulsion. That is why horses speed as an evasion. What are they evading by running? They are avoiding impulsion because it is based on working with their haunches! Impulsion represents a sophisticated, skilled, learned way of carrying, which develops as a result of educating the horse to use his joints more effectively. Impulsion is created by knowledgeable riders who can control both the horse's speed (and rhythm), and the activity in his haunches. Impulse is detectable by animated motion in the limbs, which allows slow, graceful, seamless, and effortless progression. Improved balance and athletic strength give it birth (figs. 7.1 a & b).

Those who do not know enough about impulsion think that it stands for something that can be called "activity," "going forward," "moving right along," "get moving," "let's activate," and other similar expressions. They try to show impulsion by rushing their horses out of balance, running them off their feet, and hurling them off their haunches

FIGURES 7.1 A & B *The rider, Caroline Kottas-Heldenberg, controls the horse's speed by the authority of her seat in the medium and collected trot. The reins are used differently in these trots, but always as an extension of the seat. At the medium trot, the energy is flowing forward through the reins, and they participate in the driving effort. In collection, the restraint of the reins is no more than the restraint transferred from the abdominal grid and the isometric closures of the upper legs. This combination of isometric resistance effectively increases the "brakes" on the horse by increasing the downward, vertical pressure of the seat.*

onto their shoulders. Adding a high neck posture for superficially contrived "good looks," this free-falling horse will also become stiff, choppy, and small striding with mincing movements. With the combination of exchanging superficial "form" for genuine substance, a false sense of impulsion is produced by the rider that forces rushing. As a consequence, a jarring motion develops, which breaks the horse down and traumatizes the rider who is trying to cope with the rough gaits by bouncing his head, arms, elbows, and fists, and is doing anything he can to cushion the blows the horse's gait delivers.

The truth is that only through slowness (at first, very slow), while keeping the haunches active, can the rider teach the horse the engagement of his haunches. By schooling in slow rhythm, the rider can give the horse the experience of progressing through space by increased articulation (flexing and rotating) of his joints. In this way, the horse learns that he cannot avoid working with his haunches by hurling himself into a free-fall mode when responding to his rider's forward driving aids. "Forward" refers not to speed, but to the placement of the pelvis and the hocks to allow the lowering of the croup and to facilitate the horse's crouching down toward the ground. The development of strength, skill, and suppleness of the joints promotes a "soft landing" on the limbs that now can yield softly toward the ground at the time of impact with it. The rider should school the horse to understand that it is more efficient to move slowly and shift his balance toward the haunches.

As a result of driving the haunches yet slowing the forehand, the rider should convey to the horse that his goal is an unequal progression of a relatively slow forehand, with the activation of the haunches being spent on assuming increased weight on them (collection), rather than faster transportation. The rider has to school the horse to understand that energizing the haunches is not a signal for hurried transportation, but rather a request for the creation of a specific posture that can support more weight in the hindquarters. Schooling horses in this understanding of the driving aids promotes impulsion and will advance the development of collection, rather than being squandered on speed. Moving in a slow rhythm with increased activity in the haunches (done at the beginning of schooling) will help to induce the rotation and flexion of the horse's joints. This enables the horse to lift and carry his rider effortlessly.

Horses would never "discover" impulsion by themselves because nature made them animals of flight. When prompted to move, they do it swiftly by pushing (rather than lifting) themselves; they utilize their heavy forehand to propel themselves ahead with their body weight hurled forward to assist in speed. Horses naturally move by using their falling weight. This is what the culture and intelligence of the rider has to supplant with the *educated movement of impulsion*.

When great impulsion allows for engagement, we can walk alongside horses that are at a collected canter, collected trot, or passage, and the horse will not leave us behind.

Those who try for "impulsion" by chasing the horse get the *opposite of educated movement*. Instead, they promote the deterioration of energy, destruction of the gaits, and an upset of the balance.

Collection

The therapeutic work necessary for all horses to carry the rider effortlessly is the improvement of impulsion and collection. Impulsion was discussed in the last section and its twin, collection, needs discussion now. Impulsion and collection can be thought of as twin concepts because they both depend on the evolution of the horse's ambidexterity.

Equally fascinating to these twin concepts is that while working on improving impulsion and collection the rider must promote straightness, spinal alignment, the even loading of the hind legs, and the maintenance of their direction striding toward the forehand on the corresponding side.

As stated earlier, collection is the effort of the rider to shift the center of gravity toward the horse's haunches, followed by the ability of the horse to carry more weight on the hindquarters. In addition to the importance of promoting the horse's ambidexterity, another concept, that of the "closed horse," is at the heart of successful collection (figs. 7.2 a & b).

The "Closed" Horse

The major training goals, as we have seen, include the amplification of the gaits, and the collection of the horse's weight toward the haunches. In order to do that, horses should be first ridden extremely slowly, later just slowly, in order to "close" the horse. Only horses compelled to move very slowly, yet urged to maintain activity with the haunches, can develop the strength and skill necessary for collection. Closing the horse cannot be done from front to back. That is, shortening the reins to pull on them and confining the horse's neck will not result in collection. The horse in training should become very vigorous and very active in his haunches, without speeding up in order to compress himself. This is a lesson we need to teach horses— they do not know how to discover it themselves. A horse that has the right compression compresses from behind forward by tucking the lumbar back, tilting the pelvis

FIG 7.2 A   FIG 7.2 B

FIGURES 7.2 A & B *Ambidexterity is maintained by a rider's balance and posture. These pictures illustrate the author's posture. Notice how the shoulders, through the upper arms, stabilize the elbows. The vertical weight vector defines the meaning of the rider's seat, and presents the bridle to the horse. The more adhesively the rider sits, the more efficiently the horse can raise his back. A steady seat, like a suction-cup, is reliable and seems weightless to the horse. The seat should become an integral part of the horse's locomotion moving with the horse's back motion. More than just being adhesive, the seat must follow precisely by fitting into the horse's motion. A rider should not sit "on the horse," but rather "in his movement." A seat that jolts loose and breaks the continuum of adherence will be become burdensome, heavy, badly balanced, and hard to carry. The neck and poll should be carried by the horse, and not set by the rider's hands.*

forward, and sinking in the hip and croup downward. If the horse responds to leg aids by running, the schooling was incorrect, and the aiding system has broken down. Leg stimulation of energy should result in increased articulation of the joints and activity with increased engagement of the haunches.

The other compression is lateral and is equally important in bringing the haunches from the outside hind leg toward the inside shoulder. The exercises: half-pass, half-pirouette, and haunches-in facilitate this closure of the horse. If a horse travels straight, the right hock and the left knee are at a certain distance. During the three above-mentioned exercises schooled correctly, the right hock and the left knee work closer together and help compact the horse for a more collected balance. Closing a horse is analogous, in human terms, to making him squat. A rider who cannot control the horse's shoulders will let the horse fall out on them, that is, escaping alignment and functional straightening.

The shoulder should not travel at the same rate as the haunches. It has become fashionable to use German expressions to gain prestige and show that we are "dressage wise." As if English were insufficient to convey ideas that were to be invested with mystique, "the closed horse" in German is the gesschlossenes Pferd.

We often hear the chanting to ride a horse from the inside leg to the outside rein. This is suitable advice only to horses that have been straightened, made ambidextrous, through a long period of impeccable gymnastic work. Horses still crooked will not compress or "close" their action from excessive use of the inside leg and outside rein, but will instead evade work in a poor leg-yield, escaping stiffly sideways. Riding a horse from the inside leg to the outside rein is inappropriate on an unprepared horse that has not become straight enough to assume collection over the haunches. Furthermore, even a horse ready for the task of collection and engagement should contact the outside rein and slightly slacken the inside one by moving into a compacted posture with bent spinal alignment. Better attention should be paid to the rider's outside leg, which must always be positioned back behind the position of the inside leg in order to keep the horse's haunches closed. Without the outside leg back, there is no closure of the horse. The outside leg can stay back and command engagement only if the ankle is flexible keeping the heel down and the calf stretched.

To achieve better skills for closing the horse behind, a rider can do what I call the "coil exercises." In these exercises, we position the horse, for example, on a right circle. The rider places his left leg back, the right hip forward, inward, and toward the withers. Positioning is more than bending; it is properly bending a horse with his poll lowered. Positioning is bend with postural change involving a deeper poll (figs. 7.3 a & b).

After positioning and coiling the horse to the right, change direction and coil the horse counter-bent. When he engages and collects, and flexes his hips, you can then change him over to the left circle with a left bend. Then the rider can coil into a left circle, change rein in counter bending, and upon collection change to true bending on the left circle.

This exercise is similar to riding a serpentine, on which each turn starts with a counter flexion and a counter positioning. The rider's leg positioning is changed appropriately, alternating from left back on a right circle and right back on a left circle.

The outside leg is the guardian of the closing of the horse and that is why it should not move to create rhythm and impulsion. The inside leg of the rider should take care of rhythm and impulsion. The outside leg is used for bending, engaging, closing the horse. The rider's legs should not work like windshield wipers on a car (figs. 7.4 a & b).

FIGURES 7.3 A & B *Arthur Kottas-Heldenberg is one of the greatest riders of our times. In these two pictures, observe his superb demonstration of "positioning" the horse's neck. Positioning includes bending the neck, and you can do it without necessarily bending the rest of the horse's body. However, you cannot bend the horse's body without positioning the neck. From the rider's point of view, a well-positioned neck should feel bent, and hang loosely with the outside, longer neck muscle hiding the horse's eye. On the inside, contracting side of the neck, there should be a visible delineation of the flexed upper neck muscles from which the head hangs, relaxed from a soft, more deeply positioned poll. The haunches "stepping through a liquid neck" add to the positioning. Subtle contact proves that the hind legs are free to step through a rounded and elevated back. Positioning allows the horse to remain aligned in the spine, which allows even movement of his limbs as well as supple articulation of his joints when he moves on a curved pattern. Positioning brings "the shock absorbers" of the horse into play, allowing him to move through bent lines without losing impulsion or balance, or damaging the purity of his gaits. Observe this rider's outside leg positioned behind his inside leg, which keeps the horse "closed laterally" behind, and "compresses" the haunches. This prevents the haunches from falling out, and the croup from stiffening and rising up. The inside rein is used as an indirect rein—its direction is inward and upward toward the withers. The outside rein, as always, is a direct rein, which defines the amount of the horse's bending and positioning, and guards against the horse "escaping on the outside shoulder."*

FIGURES 7.4 A *Using the outside leg and outside rein straightens and bends the horse. The author is riding a horse that is tracking straight, but positioned through the neck in preparation for bending. This is called "functional straightness." The outside rein determines the degree of positioning and prevents the outside shoulder from escaping.*

FIGURES 7.4 B *The rider's outside leg is stretched further back in order to close the horse's haunches. The horse's poll is higher than it was in 7.4 A. When positioning the horse and he is still tracking straight, bend the neck with the poll lowered. You should not pull the inside rein or the horse could over-flex, lose freedom of his haunches, and as a result, go behind the bit.*

Chapter 8
Athletic Development

Suppleness is the physical prerequisite for sound gymnastic development in a horse. Increased sophistication in suppleness is the proof of correct work. The daily riding protocol outline that follow fosters suppleness (fig. 8.1).

Suppleness

A supple horse is spared the trauma caused by being ridden if each step impacting on the ground flows through a "liquid body" that allows the transmission of energy generated in the haunches to travel unhindered toward the forehand. To accomplish this, the rider must elasticize his horse daily to:

1. Lengthen and shorten his posture, his frame.

When the frame is lengthened, the horse will naturally lower his head and stretch his neck. His head should move forward and then hang down, allowing the space under the throat latch to increase.

2. Lengthen and shorten his strides.

The horse should eventually perform all his gaits on a continuum of discernible differentiation of stride length. The rider can choose at will to show collected, medium, and extended varieties of the gaits for evaluative purposes. Eventually, all three required modes of the gaits will be developed with enough sophistication to be ridden in a slow, deliberate, suspended, and cadenced manner. In this context, remember that the passage is simply the most collected medium trot and that the medium trot is merely a stretched passage.

3. Bending and straightening his torso and spine (figs. 8.2 a & b).

Straightness of the torso with appropriate spinal alignment delivers its desirable consequences: *the even loading of the hind legs*. Straightening the horse in order to load his hind legs evenly, is an informed understanding of Gustav Steinbrecht's [*Gymnasium of the Horse*, Xenophon Press 1994] admonition to "Straighten and forward!" Unfortunately, too many riders interpret that admonition to mean "Run your crooked horses off their legs as fast as you can catapult them," a misinterpretation that results from not living in an equestrian culture with its working vocabulary shared and adequately understood. However, correctly understood and executed, the perpetual straightening of horses provides for their tracking with the hind legs properly in the direction of their forehand on the corresponding side. These results are best achieved by frequently alternating between riding on straight or curved patterns and ensuring the horses' spines are properly paralleling the patterns on which they move.

The Vocabulary of Daily Work

The vocabulary of daily work is a miniature version of the vocabulary of gymnastic work for the entire schooling life of the horse.

The principle involved is called in biology "ontogeny recapitulates phylogeny" which means that the "individual development recapitulates the species' development." In training terms, our daily goals must reflect our training career goals.

Our daily equestrian activities must be identical throughout the years. Only the time spent, the complexity of tasks, the sophistication of the conceptual development in exercises change. The essentials training principles remain the same.

Training should not be drilling for competitions, and should not be drilling of "movements." All "movements" are actual exercises. They are not just "to be done," but ridden so correctly that they provide the strength and skill for the horse's athletic development.

Correct gymnastic development is obvious. A correctly gymnasticized and obedient horse will be changeable, adjustable, malleable and respond to the rider's aids seamlessly without delay.

The correctly ridden horse must be adjustable in his frame, body and stride. The more developed the horse's "gymnastic vocabulary," the more advanced his training is. The success is measurable only by the adjustability of the horse's frame from short to long; from tall to low; from collected to stretched in its various parts; and his ability to bend or straighten his spine and barrel. His limb movements should be shorter, taller, longer, and more ground-gaining.

When a rider asks for an exercise, he should merely be able to adjust the "three dials" on the the horse:

1. Lengthen and shorten his frame,
2. Lengthen and shorten his stride, and
3. Increase, decrease and change the bending. The obedient, well-trained horse placed in the length of frame, length of stride, and degree of bend where the rider chooses.

FIG 8.1

FIGURE 8.2 A *Here, Elizabeth Ball is preparing the horse for a corner. The positioning precedes the bending. The neck is well-bent inward, with the poll dropping deeper, yet sustained as the highest point of the horse's anatomy. The rider's aids prevent the outside shoulder from escaping, and compress the haunches inward enough to prevent them from falling off the path of travel. Correct bending is an act of "straightening," because it is based on precise spinal alignment that promotes the evenness of strides, such that the hind legs proceed toward their corresponding forehands.*

Note that the rider's ankle is flexed, her upper leg is deep and adhesive, and her lower leg is flexed into the stirrup. Her elbows are pressed down from the shoulders, which are rotated back and down, and her hands are together.

FIG 8.2 A

FIGURE 8.2 B *This horse is correctly bent through a corner. His spinal alignment is perfect, his haunches are lowered, and his joints are well engaged. His forehand rises at the withers, allowing free-floating liberated shoulders. When gymnasticizing, nothing is more important than correct bending, except, the impeccable straightness that results from it.*

FIG 8.2 B

It is good to remember that riding straight for thirty miles will not straighten a horse. He can be straightened only as a result of controlling the precise whereabouts of his haunches and shoulders relative to one another. The rider's success in aligning a horse's spine and straightening his movement depend on lateral flexibility for bending. Frequent changing of the bend from side to side, and altering the intensity of the bending arc, enables the rider to precisely place the horse's shoulders (forehand) in relation to his haunches (hips).

Engagement

The concept of engagement is the most complex of all the aspects of training discussed so far. The term, as it is used in French and German, also includes the notions of "commitment" and "extraordinary effort." Engagement is a complex concept because it is comprised of several tributary concepts. To further complicate matters, every aspect of engagement has its own evolution from meager beginnings to complex sophistication. To add further fascination to the engagement of the horse, we must realize that it includes the horse's mental attributes as well as his physical performance. Ultimately all correct gymnastic work will be crowned by engagement.

FIG 8.3 A   **FIG 8.3 B**

FIGURE 8.3 A *shows a slightly sagging contact with the rein to demonstrate that it strides slightly shorter steps than in figure 8.3 B yet lower at the croup. Great "bursts" into medium trot.*

The Stages of Engagement

1. On the most primitive level, physical engagement is secured when a horse does whatever he is performing better than he did it before. In simple terms, any positive response to the rider's influences qualifies as engagement. An improvement beyond the status quo is engagement. For instance, if a horse trots "ordinarily" and a rider can inspire him to upgrade that to a working trot, the horse will have "engaged." As all initial energy should first contribute to longitudinal flexion (posture) and only energy beyond the needs of flexion

should be used for transportation. Therefore, forward driving should primarily create flexion before it can provide ground-gaining transportation. In reality, the dawning of engagement appears at the beginning with the primary concept of relaxation. For improvement in the horse's flexion is the first manifestation of engagement. The relaxation and suppleness that follow also become tributaries of engagement.

On the mental level, the above-described physical reaction of the horse reveals that the horse increased his attention to his rider and verified that he can discern his rider's will. Of course, these are the beginnings that lead to submission later.

2. The next stage in the sophistication of engagement occurs when a horse can prolong improved action (gaits, movements, and figures). This is how the eventual sophistication of sustained self-carriage begins. Here, engagement refers back to the earlier concepts of rebalancing under the rider and working with as rhythmically regular footfalls as the horse can be aided to perform, for example, a medium trot. Once he begins it, he need no longer be prompted, just maintained, in that gait. A horse at this level of engagement will perpetuate his performance until his rider specifically calls him to change from that gait to performing something else (a walk, a canter, a collected trot, ad infinitum).

   Mentally, the horse will have achieved the sophistication necessary to focus on the rider so intently that he can discern aids of change from aids of maintenance. Of course, the aids of maintenance always include the rider's ability to fine tune his "dials" to keep rhythmic regularity and balance. The horse, in turn, will monitor regulatory nuances. Mental engagement on this level introduces that dreamlike state in which the horse partakes in action designed for him by another, his rider, without fearing him.

3. In the next stage of sophistication, engagement is manifested in the horse's ability and willingness to perform well the "definitive attributes" of any exercise. Every exercise has several recognizable features in addition to the constant (unwavering) requirements of relaxation, balance, rhythm, and impulsion. The quality or feature that distinguishes one exercise from another is at the top of the "taxonomy" of its composite features. For instance, the distinguishing feature that defines a half-pass at the trot is the "straddling" of the horse's legs. (And not bending, moving sideways, on the two tracks, etc., which are features shared by many other exercises as well.) That is, the crossing of the outside legs in front of the inside ones so deeply that they form the letter X when viewed from front or behind. The definitive and most distinguishing feature of a halt is immobility. Movement derogates the halt (stillness). Once we understand what the definitive features of each exercise are, we can school horses to excel in these extraordinary elements of their figures. The ability to do so is engagement. If a horse performs the definitive feature of an exercise meagerly, we call his performance "disengaged."

Mentally, at this level of sophistication, a horse performing the most important movement in the taxonomy of composite features must discern the rider's will and understand his aids. The horse must understand, for instance, that the rider's outside leg back is now neither for a canter departure nor for a haunches-in, but rather to be understood specifically to mean the displacing of the haunches in a half-pass with deeply straddling legs. Of course, the ability to discern this will demonstrate the horse's mental maturity, or even "equine wisdom," to know that the specific interplay (configuration, or gestalt) of the rider's aids cannot possibly require anything but the delivery of a well-engaged half-pass at the trot. This is the mark of a schooled horse exhibiting the sophistication of equine confidence.

4. In the final stage of sophistication, engagement becomes a sustained condition of doing better, perpetuating superior work in self-carriage, excelling in the most unique aspect of each exercise, and doing this all in the best possible balance, that is, in collection. When this capstone is placed on the horse's schooling, suppleness becomes a permanent quality. The horse's movement blankets him in his entirety. Relaxation, born of longitudinal flexion, is amplified to permeability of movement that is blocked nowhere. The horse's musculature seems to be liquid. His movements are not only amplified but also seamless. With the power of the haunches magnified and the thrust of its energy faultlessly aimed, the horse moves straight, loading his hind legs evenly without escaping by crookedness or speed. Impulsion is crowned as the greatest articulation of strong and supple joints that cannot only flex when lifting, but also sink when impacting on the ground to bear weight. Mentally, the cycle is also completed. The horse's physical strength and educated skills now empower him to finally surrender his haunches, and to render his supple back to carry his rider softly. The horse's reward for mental submission grants him the liberty of effortless movement in harmony with his rider who no longer is a burden, but merely a weight. Physical energy correctly harnessed achieves its logical fulfillment in total submission to a rider who has turned from mentor to partner in pleasure. The submission of the engaged horse is not the despicable submission of a disgruntled slave to his tormenting master. Rather, it is the consequence of perfect balance between horse and rider, united in rhythmic harmony, proposing the emergence of a new entity, one born of the horse's energy and animated by the rider's insight.

Cavalletti Riding

The use of cavalletti[3] to improve the gymnastic progress of horses has immense value. Cavalletti work is not only relevant for jumpers but is also indispensable for the basic training of dressage horses. Cavalletti work is the alpha and omega of gymnastic exercises.

---

[3] (Italian: "little horse") are small jumps, originally made of wood, used for basic horse training.

Training with cavalletti is alpha to the beginner horse that learns to observe objects on the ground and obey his rider. For him it is a tool for learning rhythmic movement, greater suspension, and improved balance. Strength and skill, the twin concepts of athletic development, are both increased with the use of cavalletti.

Such work is omega to the finished dressage horse who can relax his back, trampoline his stride, stretch his neck, cadence his stride, and refine his collection and extension on well-adjusted cavalletti. Cavalletti can help the advanced horse improve passage work, or help rehabilitate a damaged walk. The correct, and knowledgeably-adjusted cavalletti pole distances and elevation is essential to their efficacy.

The book, *Cavalletti* by Dr. Reiner Klimke [now expanded by Ingrid Klimke] remains the best resource on the subject. *Give Your Horse a Chance*, by A.L. d'Endrödy offers invaluable information on cavalletti riding.

Suggestions for Cavalletti Work

For cavalletti, as for all work, the girth must be carefully snugged so that it is not easy to make one notch tighter. A loose girth is dangerous, bruises the horse's back muscles, changes the location of the balance of rider, and causes pain. Stirrups should be shortened at least two holes above those used for sitting trot work. A helmet should be worn whether the rider trains alone or with other riders. [A helmet should be worn for all equestrian activities-Editor's note.]

1. Cavalletti can be well utilized during a group class in which riders are evenly distributed along the walls of the arena. Distances must be maintained for safety.

2. One rider is named by the instructor as the one-time leader over a certain, designated cavalletti unit, followed by the rest of the class.

3. If any of the cavalletti poles are disturbed, dislodged, moved, or rolled by a horse, the riders following him must pass the unit and continue at the wall until the poles are reset and once again ready for use. No one should remain in a holding pattern awaiting first entry on the rebuilt unit.

4. Continuous, rhythmic motion, with its hypnotic calming effect on horses, is a key element of good cavalletti work, which has at its heart, rhythm and regularity.

5. When several horses are being worked over cavalletti grids, they will be adjusted to a "generic" distance suitable to most of the horses. As all jumping is "executed on the flat," so is cavalletti work determined by the correct approach to the poles and a straight departure from them.

6. Prior to arriving at the poles, the rider must adjust the horse's rhythm, balance, impulsion, engagement, and even posture, according to judgments based on the horse's natural stride, level of collection, and ability to lengthen and shorten his strides. For success over the poles, the rider must adjust the horse's stride before reaching them.

7. Cavalletti must be approached on an absolutely straight path by an absolutely straight horse for at least 21 feet. The poles should also be departed straight. The horse must not be allowed to cut sideways, or make abrupt turns by falling on a shoulder.

8. A rider should aim the horse to the very center of the last pole of a cavalletti grid and "thread the horse through the eye of the needle" as it were, from at least twenty-one feet away.

9. A horse correctly brought to a cavalletti grid will travel over all the poles without touching one. Therefore, silence is a sign of success, and the clicking of a pole should be a reminder that an adjustment in rhythm, collection, and impulsion may be needed at the next attempt.

10. Cavalletti exercises can be done at all three gaits: walk, trot, and canter.

11. Exercises can be done over single poles or multiples, which can vary as to the length of sequences to test obedience, stamina, and control. Neither extreme is advisable for the average rider and coach. Usually, cavalletti grids consist of four to six poles, or if they are set for cantering, two to four units making up the combination.

12. In a class, horses should progress on a pattern that does not allow them to cross paths with an oncoming horse. The rule is that "The snake should not cross its tail."

13. Gymnastics improve with combinations of exercises that require a horse to shift from a trotting approach to canter leaps, and back to trotting departures.

14. Cavalletti work can vary in duration from a few minutes to satisfy special needs, such as warming-up, elevating the walk steps, and stretching the back. Or, it can be a full workout, which must not exceed 45 minutes, including appropriate, periodic rest periods.

15. Sophistication in cavalletti work may depend on many components, some of which include these variables:

    • Distance from one pole to another.

    • Height of poles from the ground (may vary in the same grid).

    • Number of poles in the sequence (number of jumping hurdles).

    • Alignment of poles or hurdles on straight, bent, or curved lines.

    • Combination of gaits required for execution and number of transitions.

Part 3:
Training the Rider

Chapter 9
What It Means to Be an Equestrian

The horse is a perfect creature, an evolutionary wonder, without the rider. However, there can be no rider without a horse.

To be an equestrian is to take a position in life dedicated to the well-being of horses in terms of their needs.

The epoch that knew the horse as a burden-bearing and speed-enhancing piece of equipment, and as a great piece of technology has, thank goodness, come to an end. With it, the possible excuses for abuse must also come to an end, for these inevitably surfaced with the popular use of any technology. The past has been replaced by an age in which the horse is chosen for his beauty, energy, and unaffected wisdom, chosen by those who love him as a friend. The horse is one of our few precious remaining daily links with nature. He allows us to participate in partnership with nature. Yet, the horse should never become a mere vehicle for sport or recreation.

We know that a horse would never, without the partnership of his rider, voluntarily develop all his talents. That task depends on human awareness and insight. An equestrian guides his horse through the mental and physical processes that result in developing and refining his natural gaits until their balance under the rider is not only recovered but also enhanced. The amplification of all his gaits affords the horse collection and enables him to carry his rider by lifting rather than pushing him through space. Thus, correct riding enhances rather than breaks down the horse's natural gaits.

Horsemanship is a complex combination of sciences based on scholarship. The nature and anatomy of the horse, the purpose and goals of training and schooling, as well as the proper means for the attainment of training goals present themselves as perpetual challenges to the equestrian.

The spirit in which horsemanship is practiced determines the rider's respectability. Because horsemanship practiced in the right spirit leads to psychological maturity, it becomes an investment in leadership. This helps explain why the educated elite that governed and ruled European civilizations for centuries were educated on horseback, and the terms referring to aristocracy and horseman in European languages were identical. Rulers preferred to be depicted in monuments and in portraits seated on a horse rather than on a throne, because riding a horse implied elevated character, not just inherited position gained by birthright.

Horsemanship is a physical activity and also a great sport. The body carries out the most menial functions of equestrian endeavors, that of transmitting communication between rider and horse. When the rider sits on a horse correctly, he should appear to be in effortless harmony with the horse's motion, while maintaining an isometrically toned posture that presents tranquility and repose.

The rider should engender in the horse a dreamlike state of exclusive focus, allowing him to progress in correct, graceful posture.

The consequence of academic expertise, spiritual and emotional maturation, and riding perfection, is the achievement of elegance. Anything done well is elegant. Marked by frugality of expression, elegant people avoid excesses and unnecessary, attention-getting flourishes. Simplicity and economy of motion are expressions of elegance. Therefore, elegant riders inconspicuously do only what is absolutely necessary. The simplest act, from potting geraniums to pouring a glass of wine, can be done as elegantly as the riding of a Grand Prix test. Elegant people act effortlessly, living on the stage of life with ease and not burdening others by drawing attention to their feelings. Nevertheless, elegance is rooted in deep feelings, but feelings not disturbingly or intrusively displayed. The elegant rider is frugal, unobtrusive, displays minimal action, and gives a technically exquisite performance. The body of the equestrian is a medium of communication. Based on harmony, the rider's aids are minuscule and light and, when the horse understands them, the rider merely maintains his understanding. Giving aids beyond what is needed is not only inelegant, but also punitive to the horse. Self-carriage includes the horse's will to continue to perform until instructed otherwise by his rider.

Horse and rider in harmonious partnership should appear as a unit in action animated by an outside force: both of them in repose, dissolved in inner tranquility, and devoted to one another with undivided attention and concentration. The outside world of humdrum realities having fallen away, horse and rider can share an intimacy only obtained when the instincts of the horse, and the banalities of the rider's everyday life are surrendered.

Riders' Offerings to Their Horses

During their lifetimes, riders will be responsible for the well-being of many horses. Men and women were not born to ride, and we can only become equestrians through a long, systematic education, which includes an apprenticeship dedicated to scholarly work with the guidance of great riding masters. No benefit can be derived from tormenting a horse with the intrusions of an inadequate rider. The rider is a necessary agent for change and the facilitator of equine improvement. Therefore, the rider's education, the development of his riding skills and character, must precede any beneficial changes for his horses. Riders either improve or destroy their horses physically or mentally. They also habituate those behaviors and skills that they encourage their horses to do. No effect of action, and no command given over any amount of time go unnoticed by the horse. Everything that is done by the rider while he is with his horse will be remembered by the horse, accepted as necessary, and assimilated by habituation.

Riding skills should not be "just good enough" to allow complacency. These skills are the foundation of successful communication and favorable training results depend on them. Unfortunately, unwanted, accidental, and haphazard activities of the rider are perceived by the horse as instructions. The rider's duty is to deliver aids only by design and not by accident. From the horse' point of view—and that is the only valid one while training him—both those actions by design and planning and those accidental and regrettable are understood, assimilated, and complied with equal weight. Horses discern riding activities but cannot analyze, evaluate, categorize, and approve of them. They have neither intuition as to what is desirable, nor aptitude for judging. Just as they cannot discern the rider's goals, they cannot discern the meaning of their aids either. Nature always takes the path of least resistance, avoiding effort, seeking inertia, disclaiming vigor. Like all living creatures, horses understand the pain of punishment and the pleasure of its absence. Inertia without pain is their ideal pleasure.

Riders must promote their horses' well-being by maintaining their state of comfort, which measurably fosters the extension of the horse's serviceable life. Riding should consist of three goals:

1. **RESTORATIVE RIDING** is designed to re-establish the purity of the horse's natural gaits, his balance and regularity of rhythm under the added foreign weight of his rider.

2. **THERAPEUTIC RIDING** aims at developing the horse's ambidexterity. Having recognized that all horses are born crooked, usually "left-handed," riders realize that while that is expedient in the wild, it is damaging when carrying the added weight of a rider. In order to achieve ambidexterity, riders must work to:

    (a) Straighten the horse by aligning his spine parallel with the line of his traveling on the ground. To keep the horse's spine evenly bent to the curvature of a circle or arc, or to keep it traveling "ruler straight" along the center line, means that he is kept "functionally straight" as he always should be. It is not enough to straighten horses and their their spines only when they are ridden on a straight line when they need to be "ruler straight," it is equally essential to ambidexterity to keep the horse "functionally straight" when the horse is on a curved line, hence, at all times.

    (b) Load the horse's hind legs evenly by applying properly functioning driving aids and appropriate exercises. Riders must prevail in teaching the horse to use his hind legs evenly with regard to length and height of stride, and articulation of the joints.

    (c) Ride each hind leg toward its corresponding fore-hand and prevent unwanted attempts to cross over, or track inward.

3. **ATHLETIC RIDING** goals may be pursued only after the restorative and therapeutic ones have been addressed. However, while there is a hierarchy of importance corresponding to the order of numbering listed above, these three riding goals must be mixed and blended successfully. They overlap, progress parallel to each other, and are mutually supportive. The art of riding is not strictly compartmentalized. Only for the sake of clarity in discussion is academic differentiation made among these goal-oriented functions.

    - Develop to the maximum the horse's inborn athletic potential.
    - Through agility and suspension, amplify his natural gaits.
    - Increase the horse's collection, which is the shifting of the center of gravity toward his haunches in order to improve his balance.

- Improve the horse's impulsion by increasing the activity and articulation of his joints so that he can lift them as well as sink on them more.
- Improve engagement by maximizing the horse's effort and by maintaining his momentum in self-carriage.

Qualitatively Different Training Goals

There are two basic, qualitative and highly differentiated training goals that must be attended to simultaneously.

1. **The horse's natural balance under the rider must be reestablished.**

    The task is continuous because harmonizing with the horse's center of gravity confirms to him our approval of the status quo. Conversely, any shift of the rider's center of gravity away from horse's center of gravity is construed by the horse as an aid, and a call for change.

    The horse must remain in perfect balance without the rider having to pull, hold up, carry, or support any part of him. In other words, balance must be supported by self-carriage, a sophistication that is achieved by degrees. The concept of self-carriage includes the horse in balance, maintaining his posture, tempo, and engagement without continual reminders from the rider.

    The horse can be in balance only under the dual conditions of *proper longitudinal flexion* and a *hock-to-bridle-connection*. Balance must be maintained with the rider feeling merely the weight of the reins and by the authority of the rider's seat. Balancing the horse depends on skillfully blending the tasks of flexion, impulsion, and straightening, which are the antidotes that perpetuate the horse's submission to, rather than his escape from the rider's aids.

    Without balance, the horse cannot progress athletically and he will potentially injure various parts of his body. In short, balance is prerequisite to the well-being and athletic progression of the horse.

2. **To develop the horse's inborn athletic potential to the fullest.**

    This effort begins the moment the rider first puts his alien weight over the horse and never ends. Horse and rider expire before fulfillment can be claimed. The full development of athletic potential refers to an ideal that we aspire toward. We continue to approach this ideal without any hope of ever fully reaching it. The means by which we hope to attain this ideal is the challenge; indeed, it is the fabric of the daily work and the substance of gratification.

    The athletic development of horses has always been motivated and guided by their riders. We must do with horses what they need for their athletic development rather than agree to give them whatever they want. Equine wants and desires are often the opposite of athletic needs.

    The smart partner must help the development of the strong partner. The horse, in turn, helps the smart partner acquire qualities, skills, and dexterity of spirit, mind, and body. It is hard to discern which partner instructs the other, but it is easy to understand that both partners benefit from a fruitful association.

Chapter 10
The Role of Teachers

The horse is a perfect creature, an evolutionary wonder, without the rider. However, there can be no rider without a horse.

Equally important in the classical riding tradition was the respect given to riders who showed wisdom in understanding the horse. The art of riding is dependent on the mastery of correct equitation.

I have relentlessly advocated in my writings, lectures, and teaching the importance of good horsemanship and the necessity of developing impeccable equitation. I have dedicated a great deal of time and energy to teaching the correct seat and aids. Without a skilled rider, horses cannot move with pure and balanced gaits, and certainly cannot develop their athletic potential.

Yet, wherever I go to teach, judge, or lecture, riders complain that their equitation is seldom corrected, much less tutored. The improvement of their riding skills is ignored. Instead, lessons concentrate on "teaching the horse," often through drilling because the rider remains an inefficient gymnastic guide. Riders may be requested to guide the horse on patterns and make certain figures and exercises. Although the horse may give a varied transportation through space, he certainly cannot improve athletically when ridden by an ineffectual rider.

Lessons are called *riding* lessons, not *horsing* lessons. Their primary purpose is to develop a rider. Once there is a good rider, he/she can become a trainer of horses, yet often riders are asked to train before they have the skills to do it. It is useless to supply a rider with coaching suggestions for his horse's gymnastic progress if the rider has a poor seat and inadequate aids. Faulty equitation will prevent the horse's progress (fig. 10.1 a & b).

Vanity may keep many riders from a willingness to hear how poorly they ride. Instead, and unwisely, they become "customers" who buy help for riding competition patterns. Ironically, the beauty of competition is based on the understanding that even in competition, we must ride our horse and not the test. The test is merely an evaluative tool by which the judge is allowed to discern the horse's gymnastic accomplishments.

What the market demands, surely will be supplied. The riding public ought to change its market demands and cultivate a new desire for impeccable equitation. With it would emerge beauty born of harmonious unity of horse and rider. Naturally, the definition of beautiful riding is correct riding. Content defines form, and not the other way around. When a rider, seemingly in repose and motionless, presents a horse in correct gaits through varied exercises, there is a wonder about their seeming

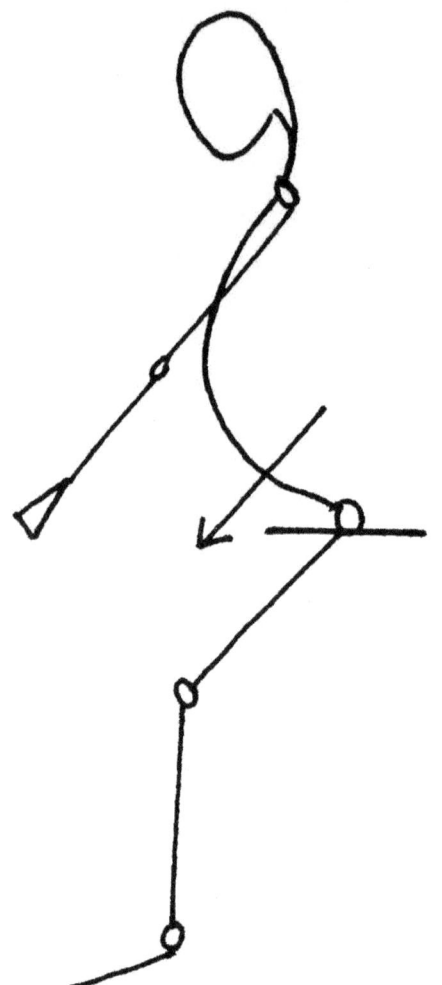

FIGURE 10.1 A *This caricatured diagram of a rider's seat illustrates some of its most common problems. Unfortunately, these problems can often be seen all at once!*

Worse still, this kind of seat is frequently not thought of as horrendously faulty, and is sometimes even taught or encouraged. This position is diametrically opposite from the one that should be acquired and developed.

Notice all of its horrible features. The head is hang-ing from a bent neck that is bulging backward to balance its weight. The shoulders are rounded and stooped, with their entire weight in front of the seat bones. The arms are stretched forward with straight and rigid elbows, responding to an intoning to "shorten your reins," "fists down," "That's it!"

The rib cage is collapsed and sunken into the abdominal cavity. The lower back is arched hollow, the buttocks are pressed back up toward the cantle of the saddle, opposing the direction of the waves supplied by the horse's back. The crotch is pressed down, and the rider sits on the fork of the thighs. The back is stiff and braced, the stomach is loose, the abdominals are slack, and the hips rock forward, engaged in an exotic belly dance. The rider's weight is falling forward and is exiting through the forward-rocking hips, never to be felt by the horse. Therefore, the "seat effect" essential to good riding, is negated.

The impossible-to-find stirrup irons, which have been lowered below the rider's foot, cause the legs to dangle helplessly like loose rubber truncheons banging along the horse's sides, making the toes point down.

unity of purpose as if animated by an external force. Perfect equitation promotes the transformation of both participants in a drama that is marked by harmony.

Effortlessness is the stamp of correct equitation, it is also the proof of a schooled horse's engagement. The longer riders tolerate their own inadequacies and the longer they are willing to toil at riding under duress, the further they will drift from the tradition that advocates the development of riders that can serve as models to be emulated by the succeeding generation of would-be riders.

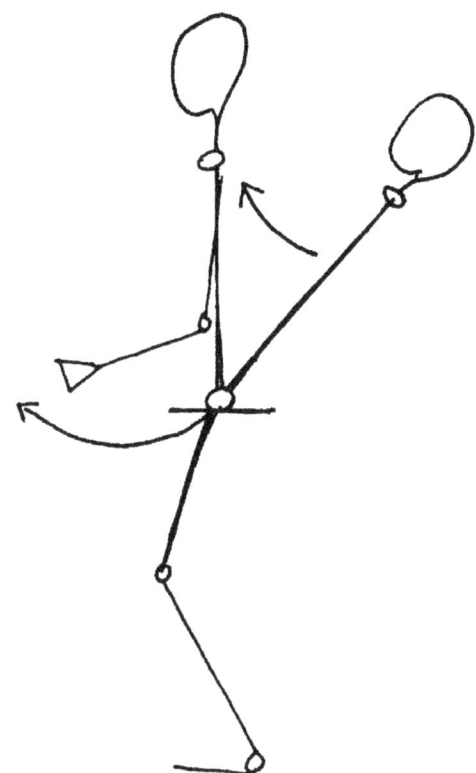

FIGURE 10.1 B *One remedy for such an extremely misguided seat is for someone to help straighten the rider's posture and spine, and hang his arms vertically down from straight shoul- ders and flatten the shoulder blades. Then, the rider's entire body needs to be slanted behind the vertical to a maximum of 45 degrees. To go beyond 45 degrees is counter-productive because the rider will jackknife. This backward-leaning position will allow the rider's contact area to remain adhesive to the saddle and travel with the wave of the horse's back.*

This position supples the lumbar back that eventually can provide forward thrust. The abdominal muscles are strengthened and isometrically toned. A vertical seat can gradually be reestablished, with the option of leaning back briefly to regain adhesiveness.

In the United States, decades of ambition about becoming internationally competitive have borne fruit. Thought, effort, resources were allocated to buy quality horses, quality coaching, and good advice to practice, participate, to be seen and known. With an equal amount of attention and dedication to equitation, horse enthusiasts can elevate their equestrian skills to exemplary levels. The best horsemanship flourishes by the correctness of its proponents and practitioners. Ideally, competitive success should be the consequence of the well-practiced art of riding.

Riders constitute a complex community of people. They represent a cross section of society that includes men and women of all ages, and of varying levels of fitness and ability. Some are complacent and enjoy the way they ride. They seek no improvement and often think that none is needed. However, a great many riders complain about the unavailability of *riding instruction* as opposed to the easily obtainable coaching. Despite differences in background or geographic location, these riders—they are in the majority—say that they cannot avail themselves of good riding instruction. Their complaints hardly vary, a sign that the need is genuine and deeply felt.

Regardless of the specifics of these riders' dissatisfaction, at the heart of each complaint remains an awareness that they have limited opportunities to learn how to ride correctly. These people are frustrated, intelligent riding aspirants deprived of the schooling they feel they need. These riders understand that without good equitation the pleasure of perceiving their horses' needs is denied.

Coaching an inadequate rider is futile. The rider, not the clinician or coach, is the instrument of the horse's schooling. Advice, however ingenious, is useless unless an attentive rider can effectively carry out the suggestions. Coaching people to ride "figures" and guide horses in competition movements is a waste of time as long as they are being repeated incorrectly by riders with inadequate riding skills. Riding faults and shortcomings when giving aids will infiltrate all rider/horse communications and diminish their validity, clarity, and value. Inadequate equitation will always produce, promote, drill, and instill faulty exercises in the horse.

The performance of any art, including riding, improves through its evaluation by peers. Should our evaluating peers be inadequately educated, we could be glorified undeservedly. It is very important that a rider's peers belong to an educated riding public that can discern right from wrong. Experts should impart their knowledge to riders in order to turn them into like-minded peers.

People who ride should focus on the joy of doing something difficult well, and should demand good riding lessons from the "marketplace." Riding is a participation in an art and sport. Fulfillment comes only by a subjective awareness of our own progression toward excellence. All fabulous riders develop fabulous horses. A horse knows how to perform well if the rider knows how to ride him.

Riding efficiency is commensurate with the degree to which the balance and the adhesiveness of a rider's seat are developed. The sport of riding depends on physical skills. To acquire fine riding skills, the rider must know what they are, how they can be developed, and must also desire to have them. Physical riding skills and knowledgeable training strategies depend on adequate scholarship. Nothing can be executed by the body, which has not first been understood by the mind.

Without the correct position, the rider cannot successfully communicate with his horse. Not only is communication at the heart of riding success, but it must always be by design and not by accident. Accidental communication delivered through instability and lack of balance will reach the horse and will puzzle him. Wisely planned and well-intentioned communications deliberately delivered are known as the system of aids. They are communications that can help the horse since all aiding has the connotation of serving the good of the object receiving it.

The correct position of the rider is best achieved by being "sculpted" by a coach (fig. 10.2). The rider should commit that position to memory and also study it in the mirror. When the horse moves on, the rider must keep the correct position regardless of the horse's motion and when successful in doing so, this position becomes his posture. Both posture and position ought to be committed to neuromuscular memory. The constant monitoring of the correct posture and position contributes to the habituation of it. In the past, great care was taken to require the ideal position from riders. The commitment to it was moti- vated by the desire to do only good for the horse. The proverbial admonition of riding humility was informed by each rider's secret knowledge of how much he failed to comfort, communi- cate with, and improve his horse.

The effective riding posture can be acquired only by a time-tested developmental system. The rider's seat is the centerpiece of the effective "aiding" system. The seat is responsible for the maintenance of balance on a moving horse. Furthermore, the balance must be sophisticated into a unity of movement encom- passing both horse and rider. The balance of the rider cannot be static. Instead, it is in an ever-changing state of motion. Much like a sophisticated dance, balance is perpetuated by motion and sustained by the ever-dynamic adjustment of the center of gravity by both participants in this dance. The stability of horse and rider that results from perfect balance of them both is also the source of predictability in motion. And, the imperceptible aids of a rider quietly sitting in a perfect position is accomplished by the ever-present minuscule movements that accompany and accommodate the oscillations delivered by the powerfully moving musculature of the horse. The quiet seat, hands, and legs effecting imperceptible aids are the result of consistent appropriate motion of delicacy and finesse, which harmoniously accommodates the horse's locomotion. The accomplishment of a

FIGURE 10.2 *The author is "sculpting" the rider. Without actually having someone put her limbs and torso accurately in the right position and posture, she cannot feel what the instructor advises. An instructor should, time and again, step up to a student [first ask the rider's permission] and then specifically place parts of the body into the right position.*

horse that moves unencumbered and in amplified strides is due to riding, which facilitates a dynamic partnership through imperceptible and appropriate motion. Both horse and rider that are united in the perpetuation of balance can experience effortlessness and weightlessness.

The balanced and adhesive seat allows the rider to sit in the horse's movement, not merely on it. This results in the ability to guide the horse from within his structural efforts by sinking into his center of gravity and working the aids in accordance with his footfalls. The horse should understand any shift of balance or any change of the rhythm by the rider as an aid for change. Random or unintentional changes in balance and rhythm committed by the rider represent a serious misunderstanding (on the part of the rider) because horses accommodate and adjust themselves according to nature's requirement for perfect balance. Rhythmic regularity is a byproduct of the dynamic readjustment of the center of gravity in order to sustain balance.

Longeing a rider to accomplish an independently bal- anced seat is indispensable to becoming a rider. Riders must be exposed to a systematic program in which the components of the seat and aids evolve through the appropriate development of strengths and skills. Much of the early development of riding skills should be honed during longeing sessions. After the rider sits well enough (through longeing) to be secure on any horse, he will be able to control the movements of his own limbs and movements anywhere in his body (figs. 10.3 a & b).

After achieving a balanced seat on the longe, a "rider" is in the making. From that point on, he can take charge of a horse's control independent of assistance by another. While regular longeing should continue, the rider will benefit from diversification. Rider diversification is possible by riding many different horses at many different tasks. Riders must be able to control and train the species, yet be limited to riding only a few with any success. Development takes place as a result of being given highly varied riding tasks, which could include riding over cavalletti, jumping, and riding cross country, in addition to gymnastic riding in the manège.

In the past, the physical position of the torso, legs, and arms was tutored with enduring patience and was repeatedly corrected until the correct position was habituated. Consequently the aids of the rider became effective, and imperceptible, leav- ing an observer to wonder in awe at what might possibly have caused the fortunate behavior in the horse.

Expertise in how, and willingness to teach the right posture and position to any rider should be the calling card of all qualified riding instructors.

Longeing is Indispensable

A rider cannot acquire and develop a correct seat and apply the aids without being longed. Even an accomplished rider needs to develop his seat and aids by frequent review sessions on the longe. The less advanced a rider, the more he needs assistance from a ground person. This person ought to be well-educated enough to pass on riding knowledge to the person being longed.

Just riding around on a circle, sitting more or less well on a docile horse does not fulfill the mission that longeing is intended to deliver. The balanced, independent, and adhesive seat is acquired through a specific, distinct set of exercises that can be done while longeing. The added skill of the aids is built after the rider's seat is well in place and together with the horse's movement—totally adhesive.

FIG 10.3 A

FIG 10.3 B

Figure 10.3 A *Longeing sessions can be done in groups. Pairs of riders can take turns longeing each other and offering correction. Every ten or fifteen minutes, there should be a change of riders in order to avoid rider fatigue, which is counterproductive. The direction that the horses are longed should also be changed to prevent fatigue.*

Figure 10.3 B *Exercises become more useful and sophisticated with a combination of arm, leg, and torso movements in a slow, rhythmic, and coordinated manner.*

Chapter 11
The Rider's Position and Aids

The gymnastic development of the horse is based on the assumption that the rider has acquired effective equitation, wellhoned aiding skills, and is in a suitable emotional state of mind.

Traditionally, the schooling of beginners was under the control of a riding master. He saw to it that pupils developed riding skills on the longe, before being allowed to hold the reins. This established the idea, supported by physical experience, that the horse's mouth is a sanctuary. The horse was partially controlled by a teacher longeing the horse from the ground. Riders were to concentrate on their education for developing a balanced, deep, adhesive seat. That is the mandatory prerequisite for the application of independent giving of the aids. Such an aiding system is called "independent" because the seat is adhesive enough to follow the horse's movements, allowing the rider's limbs, as well as his torso to be utilized at will for purposeful communication. The lack of an adhesive seat perpetuates accidental messages instead of designed communication. Independent aids facilitate the horse's movement because they do not collide with the horse's movements. The sophistication of using independent aids becomes imperceptible aiding.

Holding the reins is a privilege reserved for those entitled to be called "riders" because they have demonstrated total control over their own body. Further development of the seat, beyond what *longeing* can accomplish, was entrusted to the second stage of development, that of diversification. Riding through varied country terrain, in and out of ravines, up and down hills, and over small natural obstacles were the schooling experiences necessary for mastering balance. Tone without tension and independent control of body parts develop naturally during cross-country riding.

The Seat Explained

The seat has two meanings. One is the specific area of contact that extends from the lumbar back down to the knee, in other words, whatever moves from the lumbar area down to the knee is the rider's seat. In a broader sense, the rider's seat is *everything* because its influence is entire, from the top of the head, which should be the highest point to the bottom of the heel. The seat should be a cohesive unit that comes to the horse as a communication medium and as a transformation medium, one that is communicating cohesively and as a unit rather than in bits and pieces. Even when a teacher gives specific directions to the rider to do something with his arms and legs, those directions influence the rest of the rider's body. Because the rider is one person, he must communicate as one unit with one seat.

Riders should have balanced, deep, adhesive seats that allow them to make independent aids. Riders who remain adhesive to the saddle and to their horses do so because they understand and learned that when the horse impacts on the ground the two points of absorption in the body of the rider are in the lumbar back and the ankles. Riders who stiffen the ankles paralyze the toe outward or downward, or push themselves away from the saddle to some degree. Riders who cannot absorb the horse's movement in the lumbar back will, of course, pop loose off the saddle and depart from it.

It is important to know that an adhesive seat can still vary its pressure. When we make a transition for the horse, the pressure should always increase downward and forward by the use of the abdominal grid on a correctly working rider.

The rider's lumbar back should always remain relaxed. It should act as a hinge that allows the pelvic structure to float forward with the horse's motion. The lumbar back allows the rider to remain isometrically toned—not tense—in his torso while letting the buttocks and thighs remain adhesive to the saddle. The buttocks, the pelvic structure, should not slide on the surface of the saddle. Nor should the buttocks wipe or buff the saddle but instead should "stick to it" to allow the pelvic structure to "surf the wave of movement" produced by the motion of the horse's back.

In contrast to the loose and supple use of the lumbar back, the torso should be an isometrically toned "cabinet." The rider's "cabinet" is a complex isometric unit. For its formation, the rider should circle with the points of his shoulder back and down until both shoulder blades are flat in the trapezius muscle of the back.

This action stabilizes the posture of the torso. It allows the rider to lift the rib cage up, out of the abdominal cavity. It broadens the chest, straightens the shoulders, stretches the front of the rider, and gives him the feeling that the lowest ribs have been lifted; the waist is rendered more slender.

The rider's upper arms should hang from the shoulders, perpendicular to the ground. Very importantly, this stabilizes the arms and with them, the hands of the rider because in this position the upper arms and elbows hang effortlessly. The earth's gravitational pull places them. The direction of the upper arms and elbows points toward the plane of the rider's seat bones, and past them, to the ground. The stability provided by this upper-arm position is at the heart of riding from the seat to the bridle, rather than incorrect riding with the hands. The vertical position of the upper arms is responsible for the transferring the effects of the seat to the bridle (fig. 11.1). The firmly held upper arms and motionless elbows provide "passive resistance" when necessary. Only through this method can the rider make the correct "presentation of the bit" to the horse. By the rider isolating his elbows, the horse is permitted to feel where the bridle is when the seat of the rider remains pressing vertically down. In essence, the rider's "cabinet," especially including the steady arms and elbows, defines the rider's seat to the horse. This position of the torso contributes to the horse's feeling that any horizontal challenging of the contact through the reins will result in the rider's weight vector increasing its vertical strength. When a horse feels the

FIGURE 11.1 *To understand how to use your lower back to develop an adhesive seat, sit at the front edge of a four-legged chair, and place your feet on the floor in line with, and under your hips. Thrust your pelvis forward so that you lift the back legs of the chair off the ground. Then, rock the chair forward and backward to various different angles and at different rhythms without letting the chair's back legs touch the floor. As you ride the walk, trot, and canter, this action simulates the movement of an adhesive seat by emulating the pelvic activity necessary to follow the horse's movement.*

rider's arms as steady, quiet, and not available to jolt or jerk forward, he can resultantly understand the authority of the seat. This is the "launching pad" for success in riding with the "authority of the seat," where the reins become merely artificial extensions of the workings of the seat.

When you observe a rider with the upper torso held isometrically firm, you can understand that the large trapezius muscle that comes from the neck to the waistline is held in isometric firmness to give erect spinal column carriage. The spinal column will collapse, wiggle, or turns into an S-curve unless the entire trapezius muscle structure supports it upright, including a vertical neck, and an elevated head. A rider sitting with straight shoulders and vertical pressure down through the upper arms and elbows reminds us immediately of the basic truth of a correctly balanced and isometrically well-honed seat. The buttocks and the pelvis must behave like those of a soldier standing at attention. Everything to the point of the two seat bones and the buttocks drops down into the horse's back, and movement is as natural as it is for a soldier standing at attention. In that correct posture, the soldier does not become fatigued, even if his guard duty lasts for hours. He can walk away from the guard post without a backache or without limping. The difficult part of the rider's position to develop is from the seat bone and pelvis down. When the human leg is at rest, it wants to have the upper leg and thigh horizontal, the knee high and the toes hanging down. So, the "chair seat" is natural yet the rider's seat is not effective in the "chair seat" position. The rider's head high, the torso pressure increases to make changes and during transitions. Pressure of the adhesive seat decreases when you wish to harmonize and approve of the horse's movement. You allow your pelvic structure and seat to float with the horse, thereby confirming and approving his status quo in movement.

To help discover and develop the correct leg position, the rider circles the leg back using the stirrup leather as a radius in which the upper leg and thigh arc back and the upper leg is rendered more vertical than it was before. With the knee pointing more or less downward, the rider then stretches the lower leg until it is almost horizontal and moves the heels out, away from the horse's sides. The flat of the inner calf is returned to the horse and the calf slides down by raising the toe until it is stretched and draped into a position directly under the seat in a vertical line. Then the rider's leg is correctly balanced and continues the vertical balance of the torso. The leg has features such as the toe being positioned just under or slightly behind the knee, depending upon the rider and the horse's structure, and depending on the activity. The rider allows the leg to be draped, yet hang effortlessly without gripping the horse's rib cage or sides (figs. 11.2 a–h).

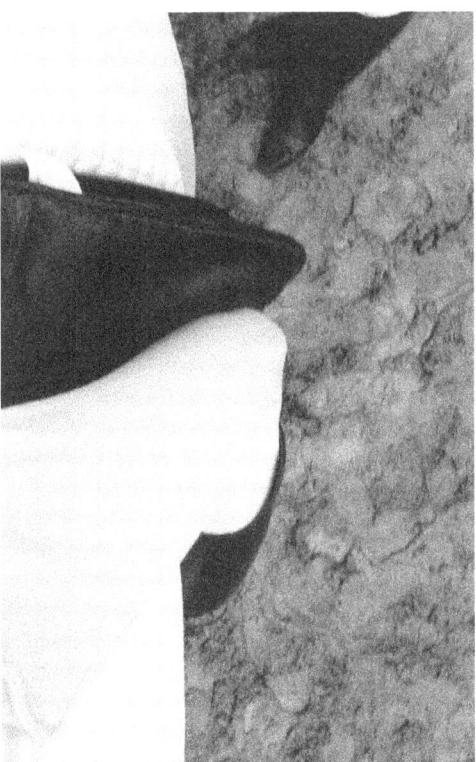 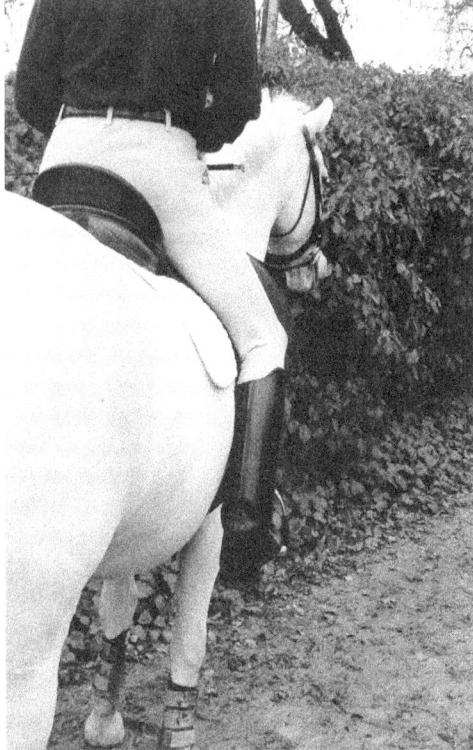

FIGURE 11.2 A & B *These pictures show views of the inside upper leg rotated inward at the knee and toe. This position allows the thigh to drape and creates correct contact for the upper calf with the horse's side. This is the key to stabiliz- ing the seat, and to preventing the rider's heels from being drawn up and pinching the horse like a nutcracker. Notice that the rear seam of the boot never touches the horse.*

FIG 11.2 C

FIG 11.2 D

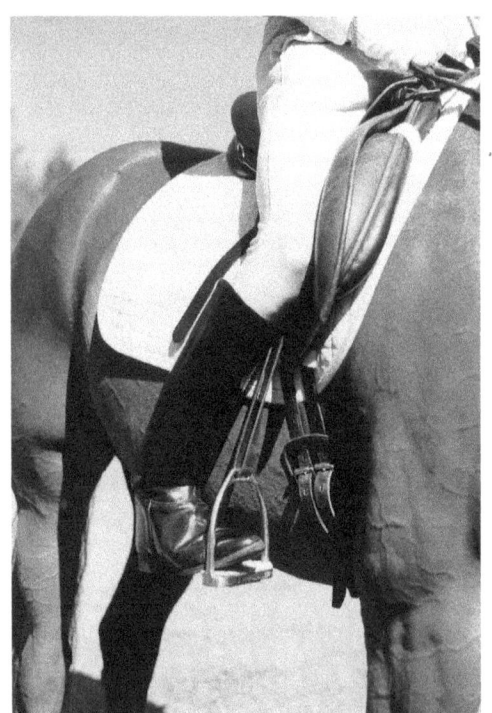

FIG 11.2 E

FIGURE 11.2 C-E *These front, back, and side views of the outside leg shows that this leg stretches back from the hip down. Note the way the upper leg turns the knee and toe in, and the heel remains down as the stirrup iron is pressed back.*

FIGURE 11.2 F *This is an inside leg position. The rider is dropping the upper leg and knee as deep and as vertically as the elasticity of his joints permit. The upper limb is rotated inward so that the front thigh muscle lies flat on the saddle skirt, and the knee is turned inward. The entire upper leg is laid down in constant adhesive friction on the saddle without the need to grip. The seat is wide, and fully anchored, and the leg is stretched into a vertical stirrup leather.*

FIGURE 11.2 G & H *These two photos show an inside (G) and outside (H) leg position. The inside leg should hang like a pendulum and be responsible for impulsion, rhythm, and cadence. The outside leg is firmly in place and motionless, which secures the alignment of the horse's haunches. However, in both positions, the lower leg stays steady because the rider has stabilized his upper leg and stabilized the knee.*

FIG 11.2 F

FIG 11.2 G

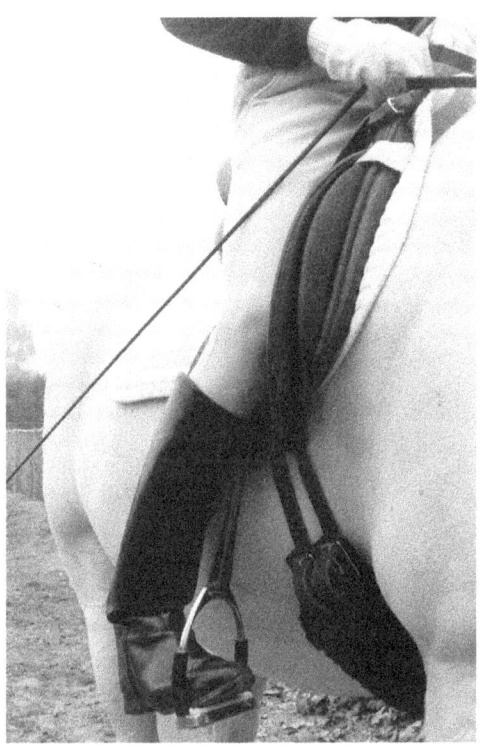

FIG 11.2 H

Each of the horse's movements occurs in three dimensions: Horizontal, Vertical and Lateral. When a horse is in motion under the correctly seated rider, the rider's pelvis (the contact area: buttocks, seat bone, and pelvic structure) is dragged forward in space from point A to point B, and the rider travels horizontally forward. To understand the horizontal thrust of the horse's movement, riders are advised to lean with straight shoulders and neck high, behind the vertical and slowly sit up toward the vertical until they feel where the horse's center of gravity is located in the vertical plane. This exercise also creates the position for pelvic thrust and helps the rider experience the horizontal floating movement of the pelvics with movement of the horse's back. Finally, the rider sits up to the vertical.

The second dimension of the movement of the horse is his impact on the ground, which gives the rider's seat verticality or the vertical dimension. With head carried high, lumbar back rendered looser and softer, muscles around the hips and pelvis more relaxed, the rider can use the weight of the torso to squish down and begin to trampoline on the horse, emphasizing the verticality of the steps. This verticality of the seat allows and teaches the rider to moderate the horse's movement from horizontal to vertical. The horse moves with alternating limb action, the shoulder alternates with the corresponding hind leg. Whether we ride straight and forward, lateral figures, or two-track movements, we must always abide by one rule: the rider's shoulders must parallel the horse's shoulders to maintain the center of gravity correctly and the rider's hips must maintain a position parallel to the horse's hips. When we realize that a horse moves with alternating shoulders and alternating hips, we understand that in order to follow the horse, the rider must also have a miniature lateral oscillation that makes him capable of moving with the horse.

A silent, elegant immobility of the inconspicuous seat and aiding system is silent *relative to the movement* of the muscle groups of the horse. If a rider is silent and motionless relative to the ground, he is not silent but instead becomes a rigid rider. A silent rider moves enough (in the legs, hand, seat, shoulder, torso, lumbar back, hips, seat bones), side-to-side in the lateral, the vertical, and the horizontal dimensions of the horse's movement. Once the rider has become an "insider" [to the horse's movement], "a part-and-parcel" participator with the horse's structure and movement, is when the rider can truly influence the horse and call upon him to make changes.

The Rider's Seat

The rider's seat is composed of his entire torso: head, neck, and pelvis. There are three major aiding areas in the rider's body: seat, legs, and hands (or reins). We differentiate between these areas because they have varied functions.

The leg has three important functions:

1. The legs of the rider are the primary source of initiating locomotive energy from the horse. They energize the horse's haunches, which in turn create

locomotion. In addition, the rider uses the leg to sharpen the cadence (the rhythmic clarity of the horse's footfall), and [more specifically] for that purpose, uses the inside leg.

2. The rider also uses the legs to bend the horse. The horse is bent around the inside leg, but bent with the outside leg.

3. The outside leg is positioned back, behind the girth [during bent movements] and creates the "closing of the horse."

The function of the torso is to restrain the horse, give him direction, and give him a place to go to. The torso also acts as a transformer of energy emitted from the haunches. The lumbar back follows the horse with the rider's adhesive seat. The lumbar back is a shock absorber as well. It allows the horse's energy to travel up through the rider's back into his neck. By holding the neck steady and the head in a high posture, the rider can return the energy down his arm and elbow and send it altered forward toward the horse's mouth. The seat of the rider is an energy transformer that, in addition to being sensitive enough to understand and feel the level of energy he is receiving, must also be able to give energy back to the horse altered: slower, faster, longer, taller, bent, or straight. When the rider gives this energy back to the horse altered, he does so through the arms and through the reins. But these must be the extension of the rider's torso and cabinetry.

We can observe the function of the torso transforming the energy of the haunches by watching a horse and rider perform a shoulder-in at the walk. The inside shoulder pivots back, but with it come the entire elbow and arm. The entire inside torso brings the shoulder and rib cage back behind the hip. This increases the effect of center of gravity down through the inside seat bone, down all the way to the inside heel. Of course, the toe remains elevated, and from that the rider gains the added energy and power of the inside leg, which allows the rider to send the horse's hind leg under his structure (figs. 11.3 a & b).

To straighten the horse, the body of the rider is used as a transformer of energy in another direction. In the haunches-in at the walk, the rider's shoulders parallel the horse's shoulders, the rider's hips parallel the horse's hips, which empower the center of gravity to remain in the vertical axis of the inside seat bone. Yet, the closing leg, the closer of the haunches, allows the inward movement.

The function of the hand is the hardest to understand. The hands should always be an extension of the seat and, therefore, can essentially do only two things. One is passive resistance. The other option is active yielding forward. In passive resistance, the shoulders are back and down, the arms hanging down from them, the elbows in a firm position, the "cabinetry" is lifted by the aforementioned shoulder position. Once again, the "soldier" is at attention; the hands are closed and that is, in passive resistance. Because the horse feels the isometric strength of the rider's posture, the abdominal grid no longer allows his strong neck to use the rider's arms as loose pulleys (as though the reins and arms were elastic bands that never have a termination point.)

FIG 11.3 A **FIG 11.3 B**

FIGURE 11.3 A & B *What seems to be effortless is actually a diffi- cult task. Riding a horse without inhibiting his haunches requires a seamless flow of energy. This is at the heart of suppling.*

(A) The author is exaggerating the position of his inside shoulder and arm forward to show that the bending on the circle is not controlled by pulling the inside rein. The rider's shoulders should always parallel the position of the horse's shoulders. This horse is moving "uphill," and well-bent on the circle.

(B) The horse is moving "geometrically" straight, that is "ruler straight," on a diagonal at the trot. To straighten a horse, a rider must sit square—shoulders, elbows, hips, knees, and ankles are evenly placed on both sides of the horse providing a "corridor" of aids.

A constant bouncing of a rider's arm and hands forward and without passive resistance and a rider's involuntary following of the horse's nodding head forward misinforms the horse to feel that there is no rider's seat. The seat is always defined to the horse by the position of the rider's elbows. The horse is cognizant of the rider's vertical pressure down on his spine through the immobility of the rider's upper arm and elbow position. Cognizance of the 90-degree interception of human spine with equine spine is through the elbow. If the elbow floats, or is in any way unsteady, the back of the rider feels virtually like a loose rubber band to the horse. There is no structure with downward pressure on him. Therefore, his hindquarters do not have a precise feeling for where to put his strength in order to find the center of gravity.

In a passive-resistance attitude, the rider's pelvis is pushed forward toward his waiting fists. The hands do not pull back but, instead, the rider's lumbar back slightly rounding, his abdominal grid firming, pushes his hips and pelvis toward his hands. As a result, the horse is enabled to feel his frame, designated by the adhesive seat and the passivity of the hands. He then perceives the rider's seat in the bit. Thus, the presentation of the bit is accomplished and now the horse can and will contact the bit with his hocks. The contact must always be by the horse accepting the rider's seat, not by a "seatless" rider pulling on the bit. The rider should merely hold the weight of the rein leathers and the bridle. The horse's hindquarters are sent toward the bit; his mouth is not pulled back toward his haunches. When the horse arrives on the bit, the rider feels him resting on his palm.

The rider's inside leg is the primary source of energy. The action and tone of the lumbar back modify that energy. The horse is sent forward by the rider's whole body, which must not act in bits and pieces. To stop a horse, the rider must not only provide preparation with half-halts, but also must complete the transition aids by passive resistance augmented by an omission of driving aids. Once again, the seat is thrust toward the waiting hands, but the upper legs and knees close to stabilize and the lumbar back drops an inactive seat down toward the [horse's] center of gravity. All transitions must be done with the seat. The reins merely transfer the accomplishments of the seat to the bridle (fig. 11.4).

FIGURE 11.4 *The author is riding a medium trot on a circle and demonstrating that this horse's diagonal pair of legs are in exact synchronization, while his spinal alignment is continuous and even. The horse is moving through his entire body, and is uphill.*

The rider looks passive, unperturbed, and projects the image that the horse is work- ing by "reading" the rider's mind. The horse is the active and strong partner, while the rider is the meditative, tranquil, and inspiring partner. The rider's mind and spirit are being carried by a horse who visibly enjoys guidance. Riding should never be confrontational because the horse is never conspiratorial. Instead, cooperation through mutual pleasure is what is called for.

When we understand the importance of the seat, we can follow the logic of a correct system of giving the aids. This means that the ***legs energize, the seat modifies, and the reins verify***, in that order. The seat determines what movement the horse will deliver when his rider energizes him. When he delivers the correct results, the rider must yield the reins subtly to verify to him that he has understood the aids. Yielding is rewarding. Therefore, it must be instant and timely, and sufficient to be understood (figs. 11.5 a & b). The order [of the aids] must still be leg first, seat modifier, hands last. We should not chuck his mouth, or somehow modify him in the front first to tell him, "Enough medium trot, now passage." We get passage out of the medium trot by touching the ribs of the horse. We still start with the leg a little slower, and the modifier, the seat, jumps in with a deeper vertical oscillation.

FIGURES 11.5 A & B *These two photos of the author show two different horses performing excellent halts. All horses should be halted square, in balance and remain relaxed anywhere, including in cross-country riding. The essence of any halt is immobility. The horse can and should be able to sustain this immobility. It used to be required of horses standing on the parade grounds. They were not pitied for having to standing still, even if an emperor or king was tardy in appearing. Horses are so comfortable when standing correctly that they can and will go to sleep in the standing position.*

On the other hand, the rider's posture should remain correct and he should be alert. Safety, age-old discipline, and most of all, a respect for the horse, demands that a rider should never use a horse as a chair, worse yet, a sofa, to sit on.

Remember, the seat has three dimensions: horizontal, vertical, and lateral. We notify the horse with a vertical punch and we arrive to passage and the hand says to him, "Open, slack open. You are now to hold your posture." So, it is still the same sequence. It is a very hard system, a very hard philosophy to learn. Unfortunately, not everybody learns on a school horse, which means the feedback is not always present.

To canter a horse from the halt, the rider's aids start from the top of the head and go down through the seat to the legs. To follow with the lumbar back, the shoulder of the rider parallels the shoulder of the horse. Without laterality in the torso of the rider, there is no collection. Collection is not pulling, collection is not shortening the neck, instead, collection is getting the horse on your seat. To demonstrate collection, the rider should be able to yield either hand and the horse should not change his gait. The rider lowers himself vertically into the back of the horse at the trot, and the horse answers by becoming more vertical in his actions. It is the same as hitting a ball on the floor of a gymnasium, the bigger the slap, the higher the ball bounces. If you make little pats on it, it is a little ball doing little things. If you give it a good bat, it jumps up. With the horse's back and stride, it is the same.

People often refer to the style of riding (I hate to use those words), as if riding could have a style. It is a science. What is the "style" in neurology? There is no "style." There is just knowledge. The "style" has changed a lot, even in correct riding. The very correct riders ride with much longer extended stirrup leathers than we were encouraged to do more than a generation ago. Because of that, we have lost many of the important angulations that were taught for the correct seat and gaits. It is extremely hard to keep the rider's lower leg stretched and draped. It is good to remember the two key words: we have to *stretch* it before we can drape it, so that it *hangs*. But the leg never leaves the horse's side, no daylight shows between horse's belly and rider's leg and yet, there is no gripping either. This can only be done if the stirrup is short enough, and the upper leg and knee are back enough and deep enough so that the ankle flexes and the toe is sharply up, not horizontal, not down. The toe-down fishing [for the stirrup] position immediately slackens the top [leg] muscles. There is no tone, or isometric possibility in the calf muscles, unless the toe is sharply up and the heel down. This was one of de la Guérinière's [*Ecole de Cavalerie Expanded Complete Edition of Part II*, 2015 Xenophon Press] contributions to horseback riding. One of the many—his teachings were the last major innovation in dressage riding. De la Guérinière said flex your ankles because he understood that it is the only way we can have a constantly adhesive, yet gently draped and hanging leg that does not offend the horse's side. The leg is placed on the horse's side like the fingers of a pianist on the keyboard. The fingers can play the keyboard sensitively into a Chopin ballad. The rider's leg should be placed on the ribs so he can play all the ribs like the keys of a piano, into a proper conversation with his horse. This art is slowly being lost. When de la Guérinière was teaching, it was centuries before a lot of people left Europe and came to America.

Now we can address some more sophisticated topics. When the rider has developed an independent seat, his job is to use the aids independently, so that every beat, every limb, and every part of the body can act independently from the corresponding part on the other side of his body. In other words, a bad rider, not in balance, moves like a pair of windshield wipers. When one moves, the other one moves with it. Horseback riding cannot be like that. It is highly contingent on the rider's ability to keep [the position and movement of] one side independent of the other. The rider must maintain the horse's positioning and bending by keeping the outside leg back and closing the horse behind himself.

With sophisticated riders, one can address the very important counter figures because they understand that "inside" always refers to where the horse's being is, where he is concave, and "outside" is always the longer side of the horse where the legs must have closure. So the rider's inside leg aids for propulsion, tempo and rhythm, the outside leg aids for closure. In the shoulder-out, the inside of the horse is to the outside of the circle or pattern. The outside leg of the rider should be further back than the inside leg. The rider should not confuse or badger the horse by pressing a lot with the outside leg. The inside leg can pivot the heel slightly out, and the toes can be distanced away from the horse's side, if necessary, to give the horse the correct idea. The old masters used to teach to remove the heel from the horse's side, a distance of "one hair's thickness".

The three basic hand positions and how they relate to the seat bones can be explained this way:

1. The *indirect rein* goes to the center and slightly up, so that the rein direction is toward the rider's outside shoulder and increases the positioning of the horse's neck. Positioning is the bending of the neck with one beautiful addition: bending of the neck increases, with the poll down. So it is an inward coil, but with the poll deeper. The outside ligaments of the horse's back are raised up by positioning. Positioning of the neck is key to the elasticity of all the joints in the horse's haunches. Riders who just bend without positioning cannot lighten the forehand of the horse and increase the flexibility of the joints (figs. 11.6 a & b).

2. The *direct rein* travels straight forward toward the horse's mouth and down. The bending is not changed, but it increases the horse's ability to lengthen the stride of the hind legs forward, and it prevents over-flexion and hiding behind the vertical.

3. The *third rein* position is the lead rein. Young horses need it. Older horses need it only for a correction if they are terribly stiff on one side. The hands remain on the same plane, not one forward, and one back. But the inside rein comes down and away from the neck to create a triangle away from the neck of the horse down and inward. This is to lead the horse inward, and sometimes it is very helpful in teaching the young horse toward the pirouette.

When a rider rotates the right leg back and the left is vertical, the seat bone in the right buttock rises and leaves the saddle, the seat bone on the left drops deeper on the saddle and points slightly inward and forward. This is the definition of being on the inside seat bone. Learning riders ask interesting questions like, where is my seat bone supposed to be when I do a half-pass or shoulder-in? The question is a good one. Just remember that the seat bone is always down on the side of inside leg presuming the outside leg is positioned back, as it should be for all bending, there is no question. Half-pass left, the outside [right] leg is supposed to be [back and] down. Which seat bone is down? The left. Pirouette left, the outside [right] leg is back connecting the leg of closure. Which seat bone is down? The inside [left] seat bone. There is no question (figs. 11.7 a–c).

The rider is always on the inside seat bone on the circle because of the positioning of the leg and the proper conversation of the leg. A half-pirouette to change rein is a

FIGURE 11.6 A & B *These two riders, Caroline Kottas-Heldenberg (A) and Julia Coppard (B), show the haunches-in exercise in differing phases of footfall. The suppling and elasticity needed to do this exercise are obvious. This suppling is possible because of the positioning of the horses' necks, in addition to their accurate bending. Observe that the direction of both riders' lower arms is identical. The inside reins are in the indirect position, and the outside reins are in the direct position. On the other hand, the rider's posture should remain correct and he should be alert. Safety, age-old discipline, and most of all, a respect for the horse, demands that a rider should never use a horse as a chair, worse yet, a sofa, to sit on.*

complicated matter because the rhythm must remain accurate and marching, and the horse goes alternatively shoulder-in, hips-in, shoulder-in, hips-in until he turns. To prevent bracing of the horse's neck, the rider must use unity of seat, hands, and legs. The horse participates in an exercise correctly only if he manages to raise the back and deepen the flexion. Otherwise, the rider trades gymnastic purity for the sake of the figure. This should never be done. The figure ought to verify and strengthen the

FIG 11.7 A

Bending the Horse

In this sequence of photos, the author is working on engaging the trot through increased bending. Notice the amount of flexion at his ankles, the stretching of his calf, and the position of the outside leg back. He is bending the haunches, and keeping them "closed" by inward compression.

FIGURE 11.7 A *The author is riding a shoulder-in.*

FIGURE 11.7 B *Riding the collected trot with "positioning." Note that the poll and neck are not over-flexed, because the "positioning" is not made by "pulling."*

FIGURE 11.7 C *A collected trot with even bending, and perfect spinal alignment. The horse is therefore, considered to be functionally straight.*

FIG 11.7 B

FIG 11.7 C

gymnastic validity. When the rider yields either the inside rein or the outside rein and the horse doesn't change silhouette, doesn't change rhythm, doesn't change tempo, the horse is on the seat [and in relative collection]. When the horse is on the seat and the rider yields very little with both reins, a half-inch or a quarter-inch and holds the horse with his seat, the verticality of the horse can increase on the slackening of the reins. This explains why we can get a passage with a slack rein. When both reins simultaneously yield, the horse elevates higher. This is a very important lesson because the horse is capable of using his "lifters" and he goes better in the vertical position. To work toward the passage, increase the verticality of the seat.

Passage is 90 percent seat and 10 percent leg. The piaffe is the opposite: 10 percent seat and 90 percent leg, or basically no seat to balance more on the haunches. In the two-track movements, the closing leg, the outside leg and the outside rein should always work in unison. When the rider pushes the horse inward, or forward with a closing leg, the outside leg and the outside rein support that action and the inside rein softens. This is also valid for flying changes. When making a flying change, the new outside leg that goes back must work together with the new outside rein in closing the horse, so that the horse changes in unity—not front leg first, hind leg a little bit later. When a rider performs a flying change, it will be imperceptible that he closes the outside leg, the outside rein. Perhaps this is so because all good riding should be imperceptible. We should not see something like a circus production, something very elaborate, but we should see that the rider uses harmony, depth of seat working down, and the change of lead means leg and hands together. When the right leg speaks, the right rein holds.

Chapter 12
Schooling Ideologies

The rider should influence a horse and communicate to him his wishes in the following order of functions:
First, the legs energize.
Then, the seat modifies.
Finally, the hands verify.

The legs can energize from different positions, in different manners and with different strength. For instance, the outside leg back, steadily adhesive, suddenly frictional, conveys a canter departure aid (fig. 12.1). But only if the seat instantly "rocks" to modify the leg's message and give it the connotation of a "strike off." Much like striking a match to light it, the canter aid must be precisely timed for the leg and seat to work together, in addition to working in the correct manner. Incremental, repetitive, or disunited aids will send the horse into a frantic trot instead of a canter. However, once the rider's communication succeeds in producing the desired results, his hands verify the horse's understanding by yielding.

We can teach only what we want the horse to do. Riders must always be careful to patiently show the horse *what they want* and *how they want* it to effect the desired results. Contrary to this kind of riding is disruptive, corrective riding. It is utterly useless for riders to stop, wrestle, haul on, hit into, saw, and jerk a horse that has not performed their ill-communicated dream fancy. The horse will never know what hit him and why; only humans can perceive "mistakes." Horses merely live on. The rider's schooling ideology must depend on patiently moving on in a fine rhythm and with friendly manners toward ideal behavioral solutions.

LEGS	
Responsible for:	**Creating**
Energy Rhythm	Tempo
Displacement	Bending/Closing Guiding Aligning Herding

FIG 12.1

FIGURE 12.2 *The author is bending the horse in a collected canter. Notice his straight shoulders, elevated rib cage, vertical upper arms, steady elbows, and deeply stretched legs.*

Great riders always appear to ride a seamless, continuous, transition-filled, and fluent schooling lesson. The horse is always flowing with his front unencumbered and urged open to forward progression, while his haunches are perpetually "closed." Driving the horse offers more seating, more engagement. Guarding the horse's bending with the outside leg helps in holding his well-stretched position. Horses should always be urged to remain "closed" and under behind by both collecting (slowing) to re-anchor them into their hocks, and by keeping the haunches bent inward on curved lines, so that they eventually "crouch" down, with the croup low and all joints sinking toward the ground at the moment of impact. Eventually, after developing strength and skill, the grounded, supporting hind leg ought to sink on its joints toward the ground (fig. 12.2).

School movements or exercise patterns should never be exchanged for the nine basic principles of riding. That is, all horses at all times ought to remain:

- Relaxed
- Focused
- Longitudinally flexed from hocks to bridle
- Balanced
- Rhythmic
- Impulsive
- Collected
- Supple
- Engaged

These nine elements should be blended with one another into a perpetually discernible presence. With their blended habituation, the horse's athletic development takes place. Ideally, these nine elements will grow and deepen in their sophistication. The result must be the supple horse that carries his rider with maximum suspension, in maximum collection and with minimal effort. Strain will be replaced by strength and skill.

No exercise should be done without the ever-present manifestations of the above-mentioned nine principles.

If a movement, an exercise, a pattern, should prove defective during schooling, the rider should improve or correct it through repetition, exaggeration, elaboration, or in combination with other movements that lead in and out of the exercise in an instructive manner. Horses learn by feeling good when they are doing an exercise well. If a horse is uncomfortable during an exercise because of strong inside-rein use during a shoulder-in, for example, he will dislike, fear, and invert to defend himself during that exercise [and the exercise will be of no benefit]. All exercises should improve on the significant basic demands of roundness in flexion, accessibility of haunches, collection, and the elevation of the horse's back. Exercises must not ruin or lessen these fundamental expectations but improve upon them.

Every ride is a warm-up ride for the rest of your life. Never do anything rash in your current ride that might sacrifice future progress.

Traditionally the schooling of riders was done in groups. In fact, group riding was not only necessitated by many riders having to train in limited spaces; it was also a means of furthering another goal of riding, the impeccable control of any horse in the midst of many other horses. After all, cavalry charges were not done alone for the glorification of the individual. Marches, parades, quadrilles, great state processions, funerals, weddings, celebrations, in addition to warfare, required horsemen riding in groups. All skills were focused on controlling horses among other horses. To be able to control a horse only under special, optimum circumstances—when alone in a tranquil manège—was not considered a documentation of equestrian accomplishment.

Riding in a formation was the daily standard. Riders were required either to follow a lead rider at a distance of two lengths (the horse's hocks visible ahead of your own horse's head) or to keep their place in an equidistant distribution around the perimeter of the schooling area. In either case, riders were required to maintain very accurate distances from one another, and in their placement within the string of horses in motion.

Instruction was not by the riding master alone. Riders' peers, by example and by pressure to keep one another in line, had great teaching influence on each other. The instructor presumed, and even demanded, that any corrections, suggestions, and guidance given to a rider, would immediately be accepted by all the other riders as if they were being addressed directly. In fact, group instruction, while highly specific in its nature, was often addressed namelessly. Of course, the instructor's suggestions were prompted mostly by the actions of specific riders. But a wise instructor choses not to name the student, emphasizing the importance of the particular instruction for all riders. All need to recognizing that no one is perfect or beyond correction and improvement.

If riders could not correct themselves, they brought down the wrath of their peers who had to hear the same instruction repeated or had to repeat exercises to suit the tardiness or required remediation of others. Equal horror was visited on riders who could not keep their tempo and therefore, their designated place in class. Peer pressure to keep one's place, to respond to instruction promptly, to do exercises accurately and well, and to progress was enormous.

Riding in a Group

The efficiency of one instructor in one hour being able to educate even a dozen or more riders was necessary in an "equestrian age." Riding skills for military and civilian transportation purposes were indispensable to a great number of people. Individual lessons for the most part were out of the question for reasons of economy. The few good instructors were always in great demand to spread their knowledge to as many of the new generation of riders as possible.

Even more interesting is the principle that learning as a member of a group is often greater, easier, and laden with more benefits than learning alone with one riding master to one's self. However, equestrian pedagogy always recognized the need for individual instruction at two stages of the development of riders.

The first stage is at the beginning, when the rider lacks the skills of a deep, adhesive, balanced seat, the prerequisite for independent riding aids delivered to the horse in adequate and timely fashion. A riding master's full attention, perpetual monitoring of the rider, ongoing honing of skills, insisting on valuable position and action adjustments can only be provided on a one-to-one basis. A most important partner at this stage of the educational effort is the "schoolmaster" horse. He calmly and patiently delivers the required gaits in good rhythm and quality, making the rider confident that if he asked correctly, the horse answered readily.

The second stage, after the full blossoming of riding skills and educated efficiency, and potential readiness for competition, riders could receive individual coaching. This should occur after the rider has acquired such proficiency in his riding skills that his training of the horse is the focus of attention.

During the majority of the time spent on the rider's equitation, even in our non-equitation age, the most appropriate way of learning is to be a member of a group of riders. The time spent from the accomplishment of being a deep-seated, balanced rider with independent aids and that of being a trainer, or riding master, ready to compete, is a time for the diversification of skills, expansion of theoretical knowledge, and achievement of camaraderie with like-minded riders in pursuit of the same equestrian virtues.

Therefore, it is for us to understand that beyond the economic efficiencies of imparting "routine" knowledge about riding skills, manège patterns, and schooling figures, knowledge is gained by being part of a riding group. In summary:

- Peer pressure is more eloquent and multifaceted than the admonishments of one riding master.

- Good riding includes not only the control of the horse's whereabouts in space but also his posture and strides as well. Holding up a class or running into another rider can have peer prestige consequences.
- Mutual observation, consistent peer evaluation, exchange of ideas and memories, sympathetic critiquing, all add value to the educational experience.

During this necessary period of diversification, riders need to "drill" and practice school patterns, school movements, and the appropriate riding positions and aids for them. Based on the thinking that "practice makes perfect" and that "one picture is worth a thousand words," riders can best work diligently by repetition, correct gestures, and elaboration (which are all training skills) in groups.

In my personal learning experience, I have had the good fortune of having teachers who found time, beyond commanding patterns (traffic policing), to expound on riding theory incessantly and as we rode, we were gently indoctrinated in the science of good horsemanship. None of this could have come to pass during an individual lesson.

The limitations on learning when the situation involves one rider, one horse, one teacher interacting, are substantial. Confounding this idea is the modern "clinic" system of an occasional visitation with infrequent following-up, which leaves both teacher and pupil at liberty to overlook much-needed corrections and an insistence on quality performance. Since both know that their interaction is limited, infrequent, accountability of both is diminished.

Riding in groups can be done in three different ways and each has its own educational values.

1. Riding in formation is done by the entire class following a designated leading rider and maintaining a distance of two horses' lengths between horses, for reasons of safety as well as noninterference with the focus of each horse on his rider. The lead rider ought to glance back when riding through corners and turns to assess the appropriateness of his tempo according to whether the class behind him is struggling to maintain his speed (spreading out), or is confined by his slowness. To lead a class takes great riding skill to effect this controlled transportation, and perpetual adjustment of the tempo according to the needs of peers.

   A special and outstandingly valuable variation on formation riding is the performance of a "carrousel" in which riders are numbered and do various patterns of great exactitude by working the even-numbered horses one way and the odd-numbered ones another. In carrousel riding, the class can be split and reunited, can "thread the needle," make synchronized turns, or mirror images of patterns and exercises. These patterns call for great concentration and precise control and give great pleasure when done well.

2. Riding in distribution is done when all horses move equidistant along the walls of the manège. Therefore, in a large area a few horses would have much more space than would many horses in a smaller arena. The important thing is to be sure riders build the skills of maintaining equal and even distances. If turns and patterns are called for, the lead rider, who commences that work, each time

will be named specifically and the riders behind him are to follow. Riding in distribution allows coaches to use larger patterns, such as circles, and allows riders better opportunities to observe the workings of their peers.

3. Riding in scatter is done when a group of riders in the same arena are at liberty to use any and all available spaces without any relationship to the position of others. It is simply the sharing of a manège by several riders who know how to follow protocol, which is to abide by the rules of behavior previously set out so as not to interfere with the riding of others. This group riding activity is best for sophisticated riders and, indeed, is the way bereiters[4] and trainers all over the world (including at the Spanish Riding School in Vienna) work their horses on a daily basis. Certainly, the values of increased control, watchfulness, and awareness of colleagues' work and invitation of critiques continue to play a great educational role in this mode of riding.

Riding in "scatter" is not just for riding masters schooling their horses, other less skilled riders may continue with an instructor. Their coach should take turns addressing the riders according to need, yet ignoring none. He can praise, admonish, suggest ideas for improvement, point out needs, help polish and perfect, or do whatever a good teacher and coach deems necessary. The entire group should listen and be aware of these coaching efforts and benefit from them, even if one is not directly addressed or singled out for instruction. The magic works through the anonymity of such instruction because riders do not feel pressure or ego involvement and can listen to their horses, although not to the exclusion of the coach.

Rules for Riding in a Group

Ride in a manner that will not disturb other riders. Watch out for the safety of others. Be aware of the special needs (for patterns) and emotional needs (for tranquillity and focus) of fellow riders. Be aware of the location and intended pattern of everyone in the manège.

1. Always keep your horse at least one horse's length away in all directions from other horses.
2. Avoid parallel passing of other horses, as this provokes horses and disturbs their riders' controls.
3. Distances can be best kept adjusted by riding deeper or shallower in the corners, riding circles, or crossing the manège to a vacant spot.
4. Do not cross the logical path of progression of any other horse.
5. Stop your horse and stand still when any other rider experiences serious trouble, is in jeopardy, horse gets loose, or rider has lost control.

---

[4] In Germany, one who has an apprenticeship of three years learning basic horsemanship and how to maintain a stable.

6. Slow-moving horses should work toward the center of the manège; horses at faster gaits should use the space along the walls.
7. When passing oncoming horses, do as you would driving a car, proceed on the right side, passing with left hands meeting.
8. To adjust any equipment (tighten the girth, shorten the stirrups, etc.), occupy the center of the arena and come to a standstill.
9. When anyone is advised, corrected, schooled, or taught, consider it addressed to you as well, and immediately check yourself on the same issue. Always presume that any instruction to anyone is relevant to you and act upon it.
10. Be aware of the work of others, not only for reasons of safety and spatial protocol, but also to learn from the ways they look and how their horses move and behave.

The Purpose of Warming Up

Any day's work with a horse is a warm-up session for the rest of his life. The principle that we never "arrive" and we never perfect our goals is at work. We seek and aspire daily for the athletic development of horses, fully cognizant that we shall never reach all of our goals nor an ideal state. Horses are living organisms that were not born to participate in an athletic training evolution designed for them by a rider.

More specifically, however, daily work, not just preparation for a competition, should begin with a period of limbering up our horses. This is more acutely felt to be necessary in climates where horses cannot be turned out and consequently spend their long days confined to a box stall. Having been intended as nature's beauty in motion, manmade confinement stiffens them. But even horses living with the luxury of a turn-out paddock need, under the weight of the rider, a period of physical "accustoming" that limbering provides. While this can be done in all three gaits, the most effective results can be obtained at the trot. At the heart of this work remains the perpetual changing of the horse's direction of going in the arena. The less a rider stays on the rail (or walls), the more frequently the direction changes, the sooner the horse will feel limber and rid of stable stiffness.

Changing direction should employ a variety of patterns, such as half-circles, serpentines of two or four loops, diagonals of various lengths, and so on. The variety of patterns can also help the horse bring his focus and attention to his rider, who keeps him interested and surprised in his work.

Limbering up should be followed by warm-up work. Curiously, this term refers to actual heat increasing in the muscles and joints by more oxygen being delivered through increased respiration. The enlarged blood vessels conveying oxygen-rich blood to muscles and joints expand them. This results in the desired effect of loosening muscles, suppling joints and, in general, a more efficiently elastic locomotion and supple carriage. Some of the most effective warm-up exercises are tempo changes within the same gait: extending and collecting the strides in walk, trot, and canter. Incidentally, these exercises will benefit the horse's ability to clarify his gaits and begin to move in rhythmic regularity, expression, suspension, and cadence.

The principle of everything "cross references" and improves the totality of performance that is correct, and tactful riding will once again be demonstrated by the results of correct limbering and warming up.

After these procedures, the horse should be ready for "athletic work" and that is learning new things and reviewing others that contribute to his skills and strength for athletic performance. For purposes of competition, the rider should replace teaching with reviewing and polishing test movements, paying special attention to the time necessary for correct preparation and transitions. Reviewing should not deteriorate to drilling by insecure riders for their own emotional needs but should keep the horse's need to remain fresh well in focus.

The principle that "the horse is your calendar" remains relevant. The length of limbering, warming, reviewing, teaching, and polishing activities depend on the horse's needs and the rider's perception of them. Communication between horse and rider should always remain reciprocal, with the horse's messages being accurately received by a thoughtful and concentrating rider.

Recommended Reading

Bürger, Udo. *The Way to Perfect Horsemanship*. North Pomfret,
    VT: Trafalgar Square Publishing, 1998 / London: J.A. Allen, 1959, 1998.
Clayton, Hilary. *Conditioning Sport Horses*. Saskatchewan, Canada:
    Sport Horse Publications, 1991.
d'Endrödy, A.L. *Give Your Horse a Chance*. North Pomfret,
    VT: Trafalgar Square Publishing, 1999 / London: J.A. Allen, 1959, 1999.
de Kunffy, Charles. *A Rider's Survival from Tyranny*. Franktown, Va:
    Xenophon Press, 2013.
de Kunffy, Charles. *The Athletic Development of the Dressage Horse*. New York:
    Howell Book House, 1992.
de Kunffy, Charles. *The Ethics and Passions of Dressage, Expanded Edition*.
    Xenophon Press, 2013.
de Kunffy, Charles. *Training Strategies for Dressage Riders*. New York:
    Howell Book House, 1994
de Kunffy, Charles. *The Art of Traditional Dressage: The Rider's Seat DVD*.
    Xenophon Press, 2016.
de la Guérinière, François. *Ecole de Cavalerie Complete Part 2 Expanded Edition*.
    Xenophon Press, 2015.
Fédération Equestre Internationale. *The Rules for Dressage Events. 20th Edition*.
    Fédération Equestre Internationale, 1999.
German National Equestrian Federation. *The Principles of Riding, The Official*
    Instruction Handbook of the German N.E.F. Addington, England:
    The Kenilworth Press, 1997.
Gianoli, Luigi. *Horse and Man*. London: J.A. Allen, 1969.
Klimke, Reiner. *Cavalletti*. New York: The Lyon's Press, 2000 /
    London: J.A. Allen, 2000.
Loch, Sylvia. *The Art of Classical Riding*. North Pomfret, VT:
    Trafalgar Square Publishing, 1990 / London: The Sportsman's Press, 1990.
Müseler, Wilhelm. *Riding Logic*. New York: Arco Publishing, 1983.
Podhajsky, Alois. *The Complete Training of Horse and Rider*. North Hollywood, CA:
    Wilshire Books, 1967 / London: The Sportsman's Press, 1991
Podhajsky, Alois. *My Horses, My Teachers*. North Pomfret, VT:
    Trafalgar Square Publishing, 1997 / London: J.A. Allen, 1997.
Seunig, Waldemar. *Horsemanship*. North Pomfret, VT:
    Trafalgar Square Publishing, 2003 / London: J.A. Allen, 2003.
Steinbrecht, Gustav. *The Gymnasium of the Horse*. Xenophon Press, 1994.
van Schaik, H.L.M. *Misconceptions and Simple Truths in Dressage*. London:
    J.A. Allen, 1989.

Watjen, Richard. *Dressage Riding*. London: J.A. Allen, 1958, 1961, 1965.
Xenophon. *The Art of Horsemanship*. London: J.A. Allen, 1962, 1969.

Xenophon Press Library

www.XenophonPress.com
Xenophon Press is dedicated to the preservation
of classical equestrian literature.
We bring both new and old works to
English-speaking riders.

30 Years with Master Nuno Oliveira, Henriquet 2011

A Journey Through the Horse's Body, Fritz 2012

A Rider's Survival from Tyranny, de Kunffy 2012

Another Horsemanship, Racinet 1994

Austrian Art of Riding, Poscharnigg 2015

Broken or Beautiful: The Struggle of Modern Dressage, Barbier/Conrod 2020

Classic Show Jumping: the de Nemethy Method, de Nemethy 2016

Classical Dressage with Anja Beran, Beran 2021

Collection or Contortion: Anatomy and Biomechanics of Positioning and Bending, Gerd Heuschmann, Doctor of Veterinary Medicine, 2024

Divide and Conquer Book 1, Lemaire de Ruffieu 2016

Divide and Conquer Book 2, Lemaire de Ruffieu 2017

Dressage for the 21st Century, Belasik 2001

Dressage in the French Tradition, Diogo de Bragança 2011

Dressage Principles and Techniques: A Blueprint for the Serious Rider, Tavora 2018

Dressage Principles Illuminated, Expanded Edition, de Kunffy 2021

Dressage Principles Illuminated, Expanded Softcover Edition, de Kunffy 2024

École de Cavalerie Part II, Robichon de la Guérinière 2015

Elements of Dressage, von Ziegner 2022

Equestrian Art: The Collected Early Writings (1951-1956), Nuno Oliveira 2022

Equestrian Art: The Collected Later Works, Nuno Oliveira 2022

Equine Osteopathy: What the Horses Have Told Me, Giniaux 2014

Essence of High School Method of Captian Raabe, Decarpentry 2023

Federico Grisone's "The Rules of Riding," Grisone/Tobey 2023

Fragments from the Writings of Max Ritter von Weyrother, Fane 2017

François Baucher: The Man and His Method, Baucher/Nelson 2013

French Equitation: a Baucherist in America, 1922 & Hand-book for Horsewomen, Bussigny 2023

General Chamberlin: America's Equestrian Genius, Matha 2020

Great Horsewomen of the 19th Century in the Circus, Nelson 2015

Gymnastic Exercises for Horses Volume II, Eleanor Russell 2013

H. Dv. 12 German Cavalry Manual of Horsemanship, Reinhold 2014

Handbook of Jumping Essentials, Lemaire de Ruffieu 2015

Handbook of Riding Essentials, Lemaire de Ruffieu 2015

Healing Hands, Giniaux, DVM 1998

Horse Training: Outdoors and High School, Beudant 2014

Horsemanship & Horsemastership Volume 1, US Cavalry 2021

Horsemanship Training Films 3 DVD set, US Cavalry 2021

I, Siglavy, Asay 2018

Journey Through the Horse's Body, Dr. Christina Fritz 2022

Learning to Ride, Santini 2016

Legacy of Master Nuno Oliveira, Millham 2013

Lessons in Lightness: Expanded Edition, Mark Russell 2019

Mark of Clover, Barczy Kelly, 2022

Methodical Dressage of the Riding Horse, Faverot de Kerbrech 2010

Military Equitation or, A Method of Breaking Horses, and Teaching Soldiers to Ride, Pembroke, and *A Treatise on Military Equitation*, Tyndale 2018

My Horses Have Something to Say, de Wispelaere 2021

Principles of Dressage and Equitation, a.k.a. Breaking and Riding, Fillis 2017

Racinet Explains Baucher, Racinet 1997

Releasing the Jaw, Poll, and Neck DVD, Mark Russell 2021

Riding and Schooling Horses, Chamberlin 2020

Riding by Torchlight, Cord 2019

Riding in Rhyme, Davies 2021

Seat, Gaits & Reactions, de Sévy, 2023

Schooling Exercises In-Hand, Hilberger 2009

Science and Art of Riding in Lightness, Stodulka 2015

Sketches of the Equestrian Art, Barbier/Sauvat 2022

The Art of Riding a Horse, D'Eisenberg 2015

The Art of Traditional Dressage, Volume 1 DVD, de Kunffy 2013

The Chamberlin Reader, Chamberlin/Matha, 2020

The de Nemethy Method: A training seminar, 8 DVD set, de Nemethy 2019

The Ethics and Passions of Dressage Expanded Edition, de Kunffy 2013

The Forward Impulse, Santini 2016

The Gymnasium of the Horse, Steinbrecht 2018

The Horses, a novel, Walker 2015

The Italian Tradition of Equestrian Art, Tomassini 2014

The Maneige Royal, de Pluvinel 2010, 2015

The New Method of Dressing Horses a.k.a. A General System of Horsemanship, Cavendish 2020

The Portuguese School of Equestrian Art, de Oliveira/da Costa 2012

The Quest for Lightness in Equitation and Equestrian Questions, Nelson/L'Hotte 2021

The Rider forms the Horse, Udo Bürger & Otto Zietzschmann, 2024

The Rules of Riding Gli Ordini di Cavalcare, Grisone/Tobey 2023

The Spanish Riding School & Piaffe and Passage, Decarpentry 2013

The Spanish Riding School: The Miracle of the White Horse DVD, US Lipizzan Association 2021

To Amaze the People with Pleasure and Delight, Walker 2015

Total Horsemanship, Racinet 1999

Training Hunters, Jumpers, and Hacks, Chamberlin 2019

Training Your Foal, Ettl 2022

Training with Master Nuno Oliveira, 2 DVD set, Eleanor Russell 2016

Truth in the Teaching of Master Nuno Oliveira, Eleanor Russell 2015

Wisdom of Master Nuno Oliveira, de Coux 2012

www.ingramcontent.com/pod-product-compliance
Lightning Source LLC
Chambersburg PA
CBHW040008080526
44586CB00027B/2925